NAPPY BY NATURE

NAPPY BY NATURE

WRITINGS ON LOVE, LIFE & SELF-DISCOVERY

CHARELL STRONG

Rasheeda -
Thanks for coming
to Trappin 101!. I hope
you enjoy and are
inspired.

♡ Cherell
Strong

For more information, wholesale inquires, author appearances, and other requests contact Freadom Publishing, LLC at FreadomPublishing@gmail.com.

First Edition

Cover art by Britney Thompson
Cover design by Cyril Trinidad
Author photo by Elijah Smith

ISBN-10: 0-692-81479-5
ISBN-13: 978-0-692-81479-6

Every girl who has ever questioned her worth—this is for you.

For Melanie, Bobby, and Linda. Your lessons, prayers, love and sacrifices are the reason I exist. I love you and miss you. Grandma Melanie and Grandma Linda I especially thank you for praying for me more than I have ever prayed for myself. I am living in your overflow.

TABLE OF CONTENTS

INTRODUCTION

They say everybody has a story. Well, I wholeheartedly agree. I just never thought mine was worth telling- or the bits that are I wouldn't tell anyone. Some stuff is just better going to the grave with you than living on Earth.

As I journeyed to become the woman I am today, friends and family tell me how proud of me they are, how much they admire my confidence, and how they wish they had my faith.

I want everyone to know I am a phenomenal actress. Proof that the outside doesn't reveal the constant inner turmoil a person endures. I'm not confident. Only recently, when I turned 26, I've stopped feeling like the DUFF, which you'll read more about later. *And my faith?* A constant uphill battle with myself and conversations with God. I've had to remind myself that faith the size of a mustard seed is all that's needed. We don't need to give sermons on the mountain top and shout our faith to any and everybody to have it. And my faith doesn't stop there. Its relationship. I talk to God and He talks to me—sometimes I listen and sometimes I don't. Writing this book, I grudgingly obeyed, because the only thing worse than not receiving God's will is disobeying His command.

So everybody's got a story right? Well, here's mine, at least some of it anyway.* Let's be honest, some stuff is going to the grave and for now I still got living to do. This collection of writing spans from childhood to adulthood, sharing some of my most memorable, laugh out loud, awful and vulnerable moments. I hope you not only enjoy the writing but can relate to the experiences or lessons learned. This isn't my entire life, but snapshots meant to blend life experiences that are personal yet universal. This is my contribution to the proverbial dinner table. Will you join me?

So here it is: Nappy by Nature. This is my truth. You may disagree, you may laugh, you may relate but you will understand.

GENESIS

By the book.

That's how my mother describes giving birth. No crazy stories of hours and hours of labor pains or ridiculous cravings leading up to my birth.

Nope. None.

Contractions minutes apart and cervix properly dilated. She managed to pee on the doctor during my birth. The one uh-oh moment, a fun stream of yellow headed straight at the OBGYN, just before my entrance into the world.

Any medical textbook in the nineties could have easily shown images of my mother giving birth. I came into the world strictly by the book.

My mother pushed and eventually I came out, looking like every other baby that made its way into the world that summer. Delivered three days before my due date arrived and an eviction notice would be placed on my mother's belly.

I guess I should have known how I entered the world would also be how I chose to exist in the world. By the book, following closely the guidelines and expectations of the world with only slight disruption. This is my greatest strength while also one of my greatest weaknesses. Consistently arriving early for everything because *"if you're early you're on time and if you're on time you're late."* The pregnancy was unplanned and I've spent my entire life planning and researching things, so much so I'll spend too much time planning and not enough executing. The beginning of my life a strange foreshadowing of what was to come.

They say I was born old. Everyone in my family does.
Came into this world with eyes showing knowledge.
Came into this world with a bunch of weight on my shoulders.
As if I knew this little bit of innocence would not last long.

I like to think I knew what awaited me in this world and for that reason I chose life in the slow lane. Life with rules to abide by, setting a standard that allowed for few surprises and less worry. I couldn't give my young parents any cause for pause or premature gray hairs.

I can't say I've always lived by the rules, try as I might. I've broken my fair share of rules and some have led to pain while others success. My birth was the start of it all, not just my life but how I live it.

NAZARETH

Grandma's hands were worn, wrinkled and brown
Praying hands
Cooking hands
Disciplining hands
Held an entire family in her palms
Grandma's hands were beautiful

5346 Euclid was the center of my youth. A two-story, green brick-house on the corner of the street. A street in a city that could be a heaven or a hell, depending on the people you asked. Three bedrooms, one bathroom, a kitchen, living room and basement compromised the inside, and the outside boasted a front porch and front yard, a backyard and a driveway. It was my castle, my home, my haven. Every time we turned onto 53rd street, I knew we were almost home. That green house on the corner was Grandma's. After years of hard work at the Richard Bolling Federal Building in Kansas City, she and her husband made a home for their children and their children's children and anyone else in the family. 5346 wasn't just an address it was a personal dwelling place, it was Grandma's house, and it was home to everybody. The place we gathered for barbecues, holidays, get-togethers and random stops just because you were in the neighborhood. It wasn't just the epicenter of my life; it was the center of my family.

To understand the importance of Grandma's house, understanding the woman is essential. Melanie Elizabeth Vaughn was one of a kind. An unapologetic Sapphire lady who taught me to be one too, and a pure soul. Much like me, my grandmother was heavily influenced by her grandparents. They raised her for most of her childhood on their farm in a small town in Kansas. I feel so blessed to have been reared from old-fashioned values and beliefs of hard work coupled with independence and the ability to own your life. Melanie was a grandma in what I think was the last old school generation. The ones who experienced segregation and were no stranger to hard work. The generation of "Grandma's House" where grandma knew struggle and imparted her knowledge to her kids. Melanie could whip up a meal from anything and she needed no measuring cup. A quick finger dip and lick is all she needed to see if something needed more salt or even a dash of Worcestershire sauce. Her children and grandchildren stayed out of grown folks business, spoke when they entered a room and knew to pick inside or outside- because you ain't going to be running in and out of her house. The generation that woke you up on Saturdays to clean the house then take you to a local activity or game to experience culture you weren't typically exposed to. *Oh, Melanie was special.*

As a baby, I spent a lot of time with her and her husband, my grandpa Bobby. My younger brother Darrell was an extremely sick baby and my mother had to tend to him day and night, determined that her child would survive. Her attention to my brother meant that my time was spent with my grandparents.

I have two very fond memories as a baby, one with my parents and the other with my grandparents. My grandpa laid me on their bed to change my diaper. As he wrapped up the process, he grabbed the baby powder. "Be careful not to use too much powder you'll make the baby sneeze," Grandma instructed. He put the powder on my bottom and out came a tiny sneeze from me. "See I told you," she gloated. It was the three of us, a strange yet perfect trio.

As I grew older, I remained a fixture in their bedroom. I would sleep with them at night, and not soundly by any means. A night in the bed with me would entail kicking, punching, and talking or screaming to someone or something that was disturbing my dreams. My grandparents complained of my nighttime attacks, but they never kicked me out of their bed. Every night I'd climb in beside them, suck my thumb, twirl my hair (if I could get to it through my scarf) and drift off to sleep between their warm bodies. They'd get up for work and so would I, watching *Barney* and *Captain Planet* in the middle of their bed while they got ready for work on their respective sides of the room. Every morning like clockwork. The smell of my grandpa's powder is the one thing I remember clearly, for he was a stickler for personal hygiene. My grandma would tell me when to get on the floor for a few minutes so as not see him changing, then it was back up to my programs or the morning news, I preferred my shows.

Eventually, I learned to use the phone. I knew three numbers by heart. The house phone, my Grandma's work phone, and the number to call and check the day's weather and time sponsored by the local bank. Every night before bed I would call my grandma's desk number, 816-936-3839, and listen to her voicemail prompt:

> *Hi, you've reached Melanie Downs. Your message is important to me so please leave it- (slight pause for my grandmother to catch her breath) -leave it at your convenience and I'll get back with you as soon as possible. BEEP.*

After the tone I would leave a message for her. *"Hi Grandma!*

It's Charell. I love you," or *"Hi Grandma hope you have a good day tomorrow,"* were the messages I left. She and I knew the procedure. It was such a childlike thing to do, but I think she loved to listen to them the next day. The only time I didn't leave a message was when she would be home for federal holidays where we would sit and watch the news, my cartoons, and our favorite, *The Price is Right*, where we debated over the cost of dish detergent and a can of tuna for the hopes of winning *"A BRAND NEW CAR!"*

My mom moved us several times but anytime we fell on hard times we were right back at 5346 with Grandma and Bobby. I had been moved from their bed to the trunk in their room. I wasn't a baby anymore and my nighttime terrors were packing a much more serious punch, so the trunk was my new bed. The trunk was essentially an oversized wooden crate that held our family's heirlooms which for us were my great grandmother's quilts and sewing projects and a few china dishes — stuff that legends are made of. The trunk was piled high with a collection of blankets and pillows into a makeshift bed for me. It was in the corner of their room facing my grandpa's side of the bed. Every night I would climb onto the trunk and they would each turn off their nightstand lights. Before drifting off to sleep, Grandma would always tell me a story about growing up on the farm, being an only child and the joy she had when her cousins would come to visit. Her stories were always amazing. She was raised by her grandparents and when her grandmother passed she cooked, unsuccessfully at first, for her mild-mannered grandpa burning meat that he ate no matter how charred. My Grandma was a real life farm girl. She rode horses, milked cows and walked to school on a dirt road. Some of the stories were like something out of a book. But there wasn't any book around that had stories like that, so I reveled every night in her storytelling.

I remember one story of young Melanie taking her kitten to school with her. She knew she shouldn't but didn't want to leave her kitty at home. She walked to school, with her cat hidden in her school bag, with her best friends, two white, twin boys whose family farm was near hers. They were her playmates throughout childhood finding mischief and fun together. Her school was a small two-room schoolhouse separated into two classes: little kids and big kids. She managed to sneak her cat into the classroom and hide it inside her desk. At the beginning of the school day class always started with the Pledge of Allegiance. As the class began to recite the pledge there was a small meow just loud enough to be heard over the chorus of children. Melanie tried to ignore it and the class continued until another meow rose from her desk. She had been caught. The teacher walked up to my grandma and opened her desk to discover the cat. *Now, she was really in trouble.* My grandma went to school in the 1950's and corporal punishment was allowed. The teacher wrapped her hands with a ruler and instructed her to take the cat home and come back to school without it. My grandma cried not only from being caught but also from the whipping she was guaranteed to get from her grandmother too for bringing her cat to school.

The stories were never ending. From her milking a cow, to tipping cows, to playing in a dark cemetery with her cousins and being scared to death, she did it all. She drove tractors as a kid and even had a pony. Grandma's stories were vivid, funny and true. Her deep voice was soothing and as she shared fond memories, you could feel the love for her childhood through her voice. She always said she couldn't wait to get to heaven to see her grandmother, grandpa, mom, dad, aunts, and uncles. My grandma wasn't afraid of death, instead she was excited about the prospect of heaven.

5346 was in the 'hood: not bad enough you would step over needles and crack bottles, but not good enough to get well-off white people to live there either. We had our fair share of gunshots and street brawls. Even though we lived in the 'hood, I was never exposed to much of it. The protection of my parents and grandparents ensured that we went to a private school and even when we did go to city school, they always kept us in line and under their wings.

Regardless of the neighborhood, Melanie took pride in her home and she tended to her yard regularly. The front, side and back yards were always mowed, courtesy of Bobby, and she tended to her garden. She may have left the farm, but she took her green thumb with her. The yard had flowers, exotic plants, and food.

One summer we pulled mint leaves from the front yard.

"Relly," she said bending down into the soft soil towards the plants located near the far corner of the yard, "this is mint." She reached for the textured green plant and pulled it from the ground. She held it out and told me to smell it. I leaned in, sniffed and looked up eyes big.

"It smells like toothpaste," I said.

She nodded and put it in her mouth. "You can chew it and cook with it. We are going to pull some and make tea."

I was so excited. Pulling mint would be a lot more fun than pulling weeds, after all, we would make something with them when we were done.

We gathered our mint and went into the kitchen. We pulled out a huge silver pot and filled it with water. We brought the water to boil and added the leaves as well as tea and let it brew. Boy was it good. It was so fresh. I let mine cool and added ice and lots of sugar—sweet tea has always been my preference. Mint was just one of many plants my grandma cultivated. She had a small strawberry patch and grew tomatoes in the backyard. She had a love for plants, and even as she grew older and her abilities faded, she fervently kept potted plants and a vine of tomatoes in the front of her home. For Melanie, life was precious, including that of her plants. Plants were beautiful, useful and a passion of hers.

5346 not only gave me sweet memories, but also taught me life lessons and practical skills.

One of the most important being the value of hard work - *if you don't work, you don't eat.* Everybody in my family worked and contributed to the household. My grandmother worked multiple jobs as a single mother to provide for her three children before she married my grandpa. She worked daytime at the federal building as a claims examiner, nightly as a janitor cleaning up offices, and in the summers at the Royals baseball stadium concession stand.

My grandpa worked at the boat for most of my childhood. The boat is what we called the casino. It's literally a boat on the Missouri river with all you can eat buffets and tons of gambling machines and tables for people to win, and lose, big time. The boat was seen as a good job, meaning he made good money, worked decent hours and had a benefits package with very little formal education required. Grandpa was in charge of moving the tokens from the machines to the back and vice versa. He wore steel toed boots to protect his feet because the buckets of coins were heavy and dangerous.

Every night when grandpa came home, he would sit in his designated living room chair with a brand new bottle of Budweiser, the brown bottle glistening with sweat, ready for the first big cooling gulp. I would sit at his feet and take off his work boots for him. One at a time I would unlace each boot, remove his socks and put on a fresh pair for him. If required, I would also apply Bag Balm to his feet before putting the new socks on. Bag Balm was similar to Vaseline, a thick petroleum-like substance in a green tin can that we felt could heal anything. If Bag Balm couldn't fix it, you were beyond repair.

At my grandpa's feet, I did more than change his shoes, I learned practical skills and set internal standards. He had me washing laundry at a young age. My grandmother did not wash clothes, that was my grandpa's responsibility. He was particular about the detergent, dryer sheets and how it was done. He was notorious for washing a handful of items and not making a full load. At his feet, I learned to match socks, finding and pairing them together in a neat ball for storage. I folded towels and sheets, with his help of course. I was folding clothes before I knew what folding clothes was.

My grandpa would work a full day and come home and do more work. If the garden was my grandmother's pride and joy, the overall yard and its appearance was his. He would cut the grass once or even two to three times a week, trim edges and cut weeds to keep his yard in top shape. He also watered the grass when needed from the hose on the side of the house. Everything mattered, in and outside of the house. Inside the house, he insisted on vacuuming, sweeping, and mopping, more than once a week. If I vacuumed in the morning and he got home and saw a crumb on the ground he would insist I didn't vacuum, and that I needed to do it again. His meticulousness was annoying, however, now I am just like him, noticing particles the broom missed and being particular about how clean my home is. You take care of what's yours. My grandparents exemplified being faithful with little, taking pride and good care of their modest home because it was theirs and would be a haven for their family.

At grandpa's feet and in grandma's yard I grew. In the house I was nurtured physically, mentally and emotionally. I learned basic life lessons and skills. I learned work ethic. I got memories and quality time worth more than money could buy.

5346 was my Nazareth. The place where nothing and no one came from. Where the neighborhood could easily lead to being a living statistic. There was a running joke of the neighborhood drug addict, an old family friend who struggled with addiction for years. He mowed lawns to fund his habit. The family would say, "*Don't end up like Kyle pushing a lawn mower for the rest of your life.*" The street could determine your life if you let it, my family didn't.

5346 was Melanie's, all hers, and when she finally moved to a home to accommodate her health needs what she hated most was that the new owners did not take care of the house and yard, it looked awful. There was no more tender loving care and it showed. A home is only as magical as the tenants make it. My grandma was a sorceress—making mint and front porch memories' valuable currency. 5346 was where I lived carefree. Where I was just girl. Where my magic wasn't contained. Where the seeds were planted that wouldn't blossom until decades later. I couldn't cash out on 5346; the wealth I got was inside of me and nobody was going to take it away

BIG BRAVE DOG

We spend our youth craving adulthood
Our adulthood yearning for youth
And somewhere along the way
Sweet sweet memories always lay

My growing up black was like a trending Black Twitter hashtag. From crazy family members to playing outside to eating grandma's cooking, childhood was nothing short of a one-of-a-kind experience.

***

Eat your veggies. We have all heard this mantra in some form or fashion as children. Vegetables are good for you, they help you grow big and strong. They are also disgusting. I hate most vegetables and though my palette has evolved, I still can't stomach the taste of most veggies. My family didn't care. They always insisted I cleaned my plate which often resulted in me pawning my food off to my garbage disposal of a brother or sitting at the table until everyone left and burying my food in the trashcan.

However, for our family outings, it was another task entirely. Often Sundays after church, we would go out to eat. You know fine dining: Red Lobster, Golden Corral, stuff like that.

This particular family outing we went to Golden Corral, a

family buffet restaurant. My aunt Irene made my little brother Darrell and I plates of food. Each plate consisting of meat, a starch, and a vegetable- carrots to be exact. I hated carrots. I ate my food and all that remained were the small round cooked carrots on my plate. I looked at the plate in defeat and said I was finished eating and ready for dessert. My aunt promptly told me I could not get dessert until I finished my food, meaning the remaining carrots. "*She is the devil. I hate her. She's not my mom, how is she going to make me eat carrots?*" my childhood self huffed in my head, because I would be crazy to say something like that aloud.

My little brother was given his small bowl of ice cream and dug in. I looked on in sadness and began to cry. My aunt was unmoved and unbothered by my tears. I tried to shovel a carrot in my mouth and wanted to spit it out.

"Don't you dare spit it out," she threatened. My tears increased the carrots mixing with tears and snot. If they were nasty before they were nearing disgusting now.

"C'mon, eat the carrots," my brother said trying to encourage me. "Do you want some ice cream with it?" I was still crying and Darrell proceeded to shove a spoonful of his ice cream in my mouth to help me swallow my carrots. I was now tasting not only carrots, tears, and snot but Neapolitan ice cream. I cried harder. I would never get dessert at the rate I was going.

My family was drawn to my crying. No one was on my side. They insisted I eat the disgusting vegetables. It was nearing our time to leave. I forced myself to swallow the disgusting concoction in my mouth, holding it down refusing to chuck it up. I quickly ate the remaining carrots trying to avoid tasting anything as I looked at my brother happily eating his ice cream and other adults doing whatever they wanted because they were grown. The only one I loved in that moment was my brother who tried to help, everyone else could rot with those nasty carrots.

My brother was my right hand. A little over a year apart we were darn near twins, and my mom took pleasure in dressing us alike. We would play outside, play video games, wrestle and argue with each other every minute of every day.

Once when we were riding our bikes outside we stopped for a bathroom break. Instead of heading towards the house my brother headed to the big tree in the back yard. He faced the tree, opened his pants and a yellow stream followed. I made a swift U-turn from the backdoor towards the same tree. Let's save time and pee outside; it was practical and made sense. I pulled my pants down and leaned into the tree, ready to let it go. My grandpa walked out onto the back porch caught one look at me and yelled, "Relly!" nipping it in the bud before I could even let me bladder loose. He calmly told me I can't pee outside like boys, that girls' parts aren't the same as boys. That was the first time I realized that my brother and I were different. Though we were the same in so many ways, I couldn't pee on the tree. What else wasn't I able to do?

My brother and I's shenanigans were never ending. Most were on purpose, planned with the meticulous mind of a five-year-old, like the time we decided to run away and didn't make it further than our bedroom door. I had neatly folded all of our clothes and we each took turns going into the kitchen to grab trash bags to pack our clothes. Our parents watched us with each trip as they sat at the table talking. I had piled our bags onto my baby doll's stroller and we were ready to run away to freedom a.k.a. Grandma's house. As we loaded up and headed to our bedroom door, our parents walked in together effectively stopping us in our tracks.

"Where do y'all think you're going?" my dad asked.

Laughter somewhere in the depths of their eyes, they instructed us to unpack and undo all of our hard work. My mother commented, "Darrell look at this folding, she did a good job." The one funny highlight of our botched plan. I could fold well thanks to Grandpa, but I wasn't making it to their house tonight as planned.

But some of our shenanigans were accidental, like the time we locked Mom out of the house. Mom had to walk to the laundry room to get our clothes and insisted that we lock the door. Somehow, we had put the chain on the door as well, because I've always been a stickler for security. Personal safety is always my top priority and this was no different. When Momma came back the door wouldn't open. I stood on a chair trying to open the chain and couldn't get it. I started crying and then my brother started crying. My mother stood calmly outside the door, only three inches of her visible through the door held tight by the chain. "Relly go get the phone and call 911," she instructed. It was the first time I called 911 and I was nervous. She told me what to say, that my mom was locked out of the house. They asked for our address and I had to run and ask mom. My brother and I waited while the fire department came and cut the chain to let her in. We were so relieved when she was no longer standing outside the door. Momma wasn't mad and she said I handled the situation very well.

From accidentally locking mom out, or stapling our fingers, getting stitches, from big tumbles, to Nintendo and WWE wrestling matches, my brother and I were two kids in love with being kids.

***

Riding your bike without training wheels is a kid rite of passage. In a way, it's the official big kid card. My grandparents' home was on the corner of the block and we were allowed a small bike riding radius. Down the street three houses, the three "good" neighbors, and we would turn and go to the corner to the end of the street to other "good" neighbors home behind us. This small area was safe. My family could see us and the neighbors also looked out for us, for they were like family and close to my grandparents in age. There was no foolishness and we were safe. My idea of breaking the rule was going to the fourth house before turning around. Every chance my brother and I got we were on our bikes riding from corner to corner.

My dad taught me how to ride my bike without training wheels when I was about five or six, and I remember the story more than my age.

Daddy took Darrell and me to the park with our bikes. He removed the training wheels and showed us how to ride without their aid, emphasizing the importance of balance.

Darrell got it much faster than I did and rode in circles on the playground pavement. I couldn't get it, no matter how hard I tried. The overwhelming fear of toppling over consumed me. My dad continued to coach me through.

My brother's successful riding only served to further irritate me, as if my incompetence wasn't enough. Darrell was gleefully riding his bike in circles. I could see him over my right shoulder out of the corner of my eye. I rolled my eyes and sighed turning around to my bike. His bike riding wouldn't help me anyway.

I was tired of falling. Tired of failing. I huffed a big breath and got back on my bike. Somewhere the oddest mantra came to me: *I'm a big brave dog.*

Why Chuckie Finster's words were the ones that I chose to use I have no idea. *Rugrats* was one of many shows I watched as a kid. The show followed a group of toddlers in the playpen and backyard of their family home. Anyone familiar with the show knows Chuckie was the resident scaredy-cat of the group. He was afraid of everything and would always try to rationalize with his toddler friends on why they shouldn't do something. In one episode titled "The Slide," Chuckie chants "I'm a big brave dog" to overcome is fear of the big-kids slide. Chuckie was so afraid that his nemesis Angelica called him a scaredy-cat and made a bet that he wouldn't be able to do it. The episode is spent with Chuckie's failed attempts at going down the slide and taunting from Angelica. With support from his friends, and encouragement from Suzie telling him, "*Stop saying you're scared. You're big and you're brave. Like a big brave dog,*" Chuckie conquered his fear and went down the slide.

At the moment I felt like Chuckie. I got back on my bike and with my dad holding the handlebar with one hand and the back of my seat with the other; we took off for the umpteenth time. I began to pedal. I leaned forward, eyes squinted, determined I would get it. Then I chanted my new mantra.

"*I'm a big brave dog. I'm a big brave dog.*"

Right foot push down. Pedal. "*I'm a big brave dog.*"

Left foot push down. Pedal. "*I'm a big brave dog.*"

Hands holding tight. "*I'm a big brave dog.*"

Right foot push. Turn handle bar slight right. "*I'm a big brave dog.*"

I didn't stop my mantra and never lost focus. My dad let go of me and I kept going. I was doing it! I was riding my bike, by myself, with no training wheels. *I'm a big brave dog.*

I am a big brave dog.

I. Am. A. Big. Brave. Dog.

It's amazing how such a small chant gave me all the courage I needed to conquer my fear and successfully ride my bike. Childhood simplicity is often forgotten and left stranded as we grow older. Hold onto that bit of innocence. That bit of belief that anything is possible. The belief you can do it, and all you need is to muster up a bit of strength. Lean close, look forward and focus, and we'll all be riding without training wheels sooner than we think. The simplicity of youth, and its ability to quickly conquer any lingering fear is what a big brave dog is.

I still am a big brave dog to this day.

***

Youthful optimism from eating disgusting food, tackling fears or even enjoying music is beautiful. There's no logic or jaded ideas, just pure innocence. Though harder to hold onto as we get older that innocence is key in life. It gives me the willingness to be open with myself and to possibilities as well as with others. Somewhere between childhood and adulthood we lose our spirit. The spirit that says, "*I can do anything,*" becomes a skeptic, doubting anything is possible. We lose our joy, our hope and endless determination that with one more try, we can indeed ride without training wheels. Remember hand clap games, jump rope, kickball and every other recess activity that brought simple joy? At one time, we created worlds with just our imagination and hands, and it's still possible to do.

On days when the world seems to be on my shoulders and the responsibilities of life are never ending, I call on those childhood thoughts. The ones that saw only possibility, endless opportunity and a happy ending. Always a happy ending.

My childhood was carefree. It was messy. It was full of scraped knees and dandelions- because as a kid even the weeds have beauty. My childhood was magical and every day I try to carry that magic with me.

Oh yeah, just in case you're wondering, I do eat carrots now. I eat them raw though, those cooked ones can still rot.

SUNDAY CANDY

I grew up in church, no doubt about it.

My mom and grandmother ensured that my brothers and I were constantly involved at church.

Even without a car, my Grandma's independence was not limited to the work day. My childhood church offered a transportation system, which was basically white vans with the church name emboldened on the side. The church would use the vans to pick up people without cars or elderly members unable to easily attend service without assistance. It provided a way for those who wanted to receive the word to get it.

Grandma would wake me up on Sunday mornings to get ready for church so we were ready by the time the van arrived. Like most kids, I fell asleep during service. But before falling asleep, I was always treated with a peppermint or a small strawberry candy, even though food in the sanctuary was not allowed. I would awake at the end of service with my head in my Grandma's lap. We would then say hello to our longtime church family and friends before heading to the van to go back to 5346.

There was no shortage of activities at my church. It was very traditional, with hymns and old songs that can be deemed churchy, but it was home and it was mine. It was a safe place filled with love. I never once felt unwelcome or less than. It was, and still is, an amazing place for youth. There was a nursery, kid's church, summer day camp, Vacation Bible School, sleep-away camp (a week long overnight trip to land our church owned complete with cabins, a pool, lake, and chapel), choirs for various age groups and school-year based mission programs for girls and boys.

It was through all of these programs I learned about God, fellowshipped with other youth, and made friends. Many of the programs included repetition of bible verses, which was annoying at the time but has become crucial as an adult to recall something that can apply to your life in a time of need. To remember a Psalm, Philippians 4:13 or John 3:16 or recall another verse that gives confirmation or strength has been an asset as an adult, though boring and painful as a child. At Vacation Bible School we pledged allegiance to the Bible and the Christian flag. Two pledges I still know by heart:

> *I pledge allegiance to the bible, God's Holy Word. I will make it a lamp unto my feet and a light unto my path and I will hide its words in my heart that I might not sin against God.*

> *I pledge allegiance to the Christian flag and to the savior for whose kingdom it stands: one brotherhood, uniting all Christians in service and in love.*

Simple, yet effective pledges reminding you of your duty as a child in God's kingdom that I still carry with me.

My church was also instrumental and intentional in showing us images of ourselves as young black children. We often watched movies about slavery, learned about the Underground Railroad, the Civil Rights Movement and more. During summer church camp, Ms. Housley was our resident African-American historian. She shared with us stories and lessons about being black and being unified. She was passionate about our history and celebrated the beauty of our past, present, and future. I absorbed the lessons yet disliked them- a resentment stemming from my self-hate and personal fears.

It was at sleep away camp, when I was eight years old, that I gave my life to Christ and became a Christian. I sat with my cabin mates in the chapel and when the invitation to join began I looked left and right and stood up.

"What has God done for you?" the reverend asked.

"I believe that Jesus died on the cross for me and rose on the third day," I said. It's what all the kids said.

I had officially accepted Christ as my Lord and personal savior and would be baptized once we all returned home. I was so excited that when my parents came for family night, to see what we had learned from our week at camp, I walked up again just to show them.

I was born again, made new. Life would be sweet from now on.

***

I pray to God a lot. As a child, He was some old man in the sky that heard me and made things happen. Grandma's momma and grandparents lived in the sky with Him. If I did what I was supposed to do, obey my parents and be nice to my siblings, one day I would live in the sky too. God was simple then, easy to understand.

I asked God for a lot of things. I asked Him for a little sister. I asked Him to make me pretty and skinny. And I thanked Him because I woke up. I prayed that He would help everyone in the world. I thought He's got the whole world in His hands so they must be some big hands. He can see everything from the sky so He knows what to do.

The older I get, the more I depend on God. The more I receive daily lessons on life and navigating it successfully. Not success in earthly terms of money but in terms of my heart. Of living for others through service and living the best life for myself that I can.

Believing in God and Jesus Christ is only beginning. It doesn't guarantee an easy life, in fact, it guarantees the opposite; that struggle and strife will come because I believe in Him and my faith will continually be tested.

I've never strayed too far from God. No college declarations of atheism due to an awakening of a Religion 101 class. No moving back to spirituality or traditional African practices. No, God has always been the epicenter of my belief system.

There have been moments of utter hopeless where I've fallen to my knees unable to speak, only able to cry and moan. Or there are moments when no sound comes out, I'm just there struggling in my head. When I moved to New York, and while living here, I have had many of those moments. Life hits you hard and you feel alone. My first few months in New York I felt a lot of isolation and sadness. One evening I walked through Central Park needing to be around people, even strangers, and wrote:

Here I sit
On a bench
In Central Park
The greatest city in the world
Alone
No one to call, talk to or sit with except God
And even He seems unreachable
I needed guidance, comfort
I pulled out my bible
It was foreign to me- like reading braille or searching for a word in a foreign dictionary
How sad and how wrong

I was overwhelmed and knew I needed to go directly to God. I took my faith and religion to new heights. My prayer time became longer, I fasted regularly, and spent more time in the

Word. I attended Bible study and young adult services to center and surround myself with other God-focused individuals.

As a kid, I was told there was a God. I pictured Him, prayed to Him. As an adult, I know and believe there is a God. I have encountered Him, talked to Him, cried, pleased, worshiped and celebrated all in His name.

I grew up in church.

I am growing in God.

DUFF

Walking out of a restaurant with four friends
A group of young boys stand off to the side
All four of y'all look good, they say
Except that last one, they say
She got to go, they say
I don't know why that last one is there, they say

I walked out last

The last one is me

Kids can bring me down
I know it's youth
I jonesed on people too
But that doesn't take away the sting
It doesn't detract from the fact
That what they said is true
At least I feel like it's true
There's always a DUFF in the crew, and Charell it's
usually you

I've been insulted. Taken down pegs because my appearance is
not to their liking. I do not respond. It's surely not the first time,
which makes this moment even more bitter, rank and foul

tasting in my mouth. I've had years of practice and know it does no good to acknowledge the insult. I continue walking with my friends. I'm sure the moment has passed for them. For me it's far from passed, it's fresh at the top of my mind. Eating at my consciousness, no pun intended. I'm thinking of all I could have done the past twenty-six years to avoid this moment here. *I should have ran yesterday. I shouldn't have had the piece of cake two years ago.* Ridiculous thoughts that make no sense. It seems despite my strides at personal growth, I'm still affected. Insults and comments still haunt me and hurt more than I would like to admit.

These kids are just new bodies for old insults, things I've heard for years. I've got stories on stories from childhood to adulthood on being insulted one way or another due to my weight or appearance. I've been fat my whole life. I have no memory or recollection of ever being small. I have always been bigger than average and definitely bigger than my classmates and friends.

My grandmother would constantly question me. "Charell, I'm not trying to be funny," she would preface, "*but why are you fat?*" Asking me truly perplexed, due to my being a selective eater with an extremely limited palate.

I would roll my eyes and sigh as a response. I was always annoyed. Most of my family is overweight and one of my pet peeves is fat people criticizing other fat people.

"You don't like anything," she would finish.

***

The first time I vividly remember being made fun of was in kindergarten. Typical childhood teasing that no one was immune from. My class gathered in the hallway making our way from the computer lab back to the classroom. An older girl across the hall headed to the computer lab stopped and pointed getting her two friends to join in. They called me a whale. Likened my weight to an enormous sea animal. I stood there with my head down the center of their insults. I went home and cried to my grandmother. I've wasted so many tears on insults.

The teasing and taunting continued through middle school. Couple my weight with teenage awkwardness, hair problems, acne, body odor and the like you can guess that middle school was a less than ideal time for me. There was a bit of reprieve in high school, but I wasn't free until college. The one moment that stands out the most was during middle school.

Catching the bus had been procedure since the fifth grade. Every day was the same routine: walk to the bus in the morning and walk home from the bus in the afternoon. I have always been shy around new surroundings, and my seventh grade bus was no different.

My mom had moved us to another new home and that meant a new bus with new people. Usually, I sat towards the front of the bus with my friend, Justine, keeping the tradition of being the boring, smart, fat girl. The cool kids sat in the back of the bus, which I believe is typical protocol across America. Every day they yelled, laughed, and harassed people. Fortunately, I had managed to slip under their radar.

One afternoon, the bus was extremely crowded. My friend Justine and I had no choice but to sit in the back. After we sat down, one of the popular girls came over to us.

"You need to move. This is my seat," she demanded.

I didn't respond. I looked at the seat in front of me too intimidated to speak. I didn't move one muscle.

"Fine then, ignore me, you fat cow," the eighth grader howled.

She took the seat behind me with her friend. The power the girl had was remarkable, in just a few minutes she managed to convince all of her friends in the back to hate me. All the eighth graders began to throw balls of paper at me. I tried to ignore them, but it didn't work.

I turned and yelled with a lump in my throat, trying to hold back tears, "Leave me alone!"

The kids all laughed at my pathetic attempt to defend myself. Yelling only made the torture worse. They touched my hair and called me names. Soon the bus arrived at our stop. I had the misfortune of living in the same apartment complex as most of the eighth graders. I began to cry. Hot tears streaming from my face like a faucet. Crying only seemed to strengthen the students, empowering them further. Chants came at me like bullets I couldn't dodge.

"Shrek look alike..."

"You ogre go home and cry to your mommy."

"Nappy head..."

It appeared everything they said was true. I was fat, and my hair was nappy. I walked home in tears with the sounds of Shrek and ogre ringing in my ears. That night I looked in the mirror and saw everything wrong with me.

It feels like I've been trying to outrun that moment for most of my life. Working hard to prove that I am not Shrek. Funny how childhood moments linger and define us more than we ever thought they could. They stick to us. Internal scars that never really scabbed over and healed properly.

***

In high school, I had a t-shirt I found at J.C. Penney outlet. I convinced my Grandma to buy it and one day I finally had the guts to wear it out. The shirt was black with simple white writing on it that read: *Fat People are Harder to Kidnap.* I received quite a few smiles and comments. I had figured it out— acknowledge it before anyone else does, that's the key.

I began to use my weight as a shield. To compensate for my weight, I often opted for humor making myself the butt of the joke before anyone else had the opportunity to. If I could beat them to the punch line, it would somehow soften the blow.

Right?

Wrong.

At 25, I realized how wrong I had been.

My friend Lauryn and I were going boat riding, the kind of boat that is propelled by pedaling. But first, since neither of us could swim, we went to get life jackets. After seeing only small sizes I made my usual offhand comment, this one being, "I need a fat one. I don't see it yet."

Lauryn exasperated said, "I hate when you do that."

I was stunned and taken aback. How dare she be offended? Never had anyone ever said anything about my self-deprecating comments. I reasoned that she just didn't understand. She's beautiful, with long curly hair and a curvy figure. She's never been fat, she's never been called nappy. Never been called Shrek while pieces of paper were hurled at her. Her offense was like an insult to me. Self-deprecation came as easy as breathing, and it was a shield, albeit a weak one, for my insecurities.

In order to not look like an ogre to the world, I had to abide by rules, made up things. Rules that were completely ridiculous:

1. **Two fat people cannot sit together.** Why you may ask, because we would look like one giant person. Why torture ourselves or the world like that?
2. **Don't get caught eating too much food.** Hide it, scarf it, or just do it in private.
3. **Always talk about how you plan on losing weight.**
4. **Lie about your weight.** No one but you needs to know the exact number on the scale.
5. **Always insult yourself before someone else gets the chance to.**

Seems ridiculous doesn't it? Lauryn's comment was a gut check. I had to evaluate myself. I had leaned on the crutch so long I could not stand without it, afraid that someone else would knock me off my feet if given the chance.

As if society and social encounters weren't enough shopping only added to the overwhelming hatred I already had for myself. Finding clothes is hard and finding fashionable clothes was impossible. Many shopping trips have ended in tears, sadness, self-hate and the always firm statement that I'm going on a diet.

In high school shopping for homecoming and prom dresses was always the worst. Catherine's, a store targeted at older women, was where I shopped while my friends had a plethora of options for teens and tweens. Torrid was still fairly new and their dress game was hit or miss, it still is. I often settled, my Momma and me, at an impasse. We would be fed up shopping and fed up with each other. To top it off, we had financial struggles. We had a tight budget but my mom always strived to make the most of everything- her baby would be at the dance and be beautiful.

May 2016 a young woman's prom picture went viral. The photo featured a 17 year old Tayja Jones walking out of her home heading to prom. She was big, dark-skinned with long hair and a silver sequined dress. She was harshly criticized for her weight and appearance. Internet users widely shared her picture hundreds of thousands of times with each share inciting negative comments and insults. Interestingly enough, the first thing I thought when I saw the picture was how cute her dress was. I wish they had dresses like that when I attended high school; I want a redo.

There must be an unwritten law somewhere that says if you're fat you can't be fashionable. It seems I could never find cute clothes like my friends. Shopping with them would be depressing, you can only help other people for so long, right?

Today, a lot of stores have added extended sizes, confirming there is a viable plus size market to be tapped into. However, more still needs to be done. Often these extended sizes are only available online and don't cater to women over a size 24. I would like to go in a store and try on clothes too, see how they fit and have an enjoyable shopping experience- that would be nice. It's little things like not being able to walk into a mall and have options that are frustrating.

I know what you may be thinking. *If you're so unhappy why don't you lose weight? That's the problem with fat people they eat and complain instead of getting off the couch.* Here's the issue. So often people fail to realize being fat is to be seen as less than in society. Your weight seems to make you visible to the world and invisible at the same time. You are judged based on your appearance as if your abilities are tied to your waistline. I've lost and gained more weight than I care to admit and I can say that when I've lost weight, I've received more positive reception from the public. It's so subconscious people probably don't even realize they do it. Much like I wonder if interactions are based on my gender or skin, my size has often been something I've questioned as well. Think about it, do you have inherent biases towards heavier people? What are they? That they are lazy, unhealthy and spend all day eating?

But I'm not free from this bias either. Why do I want to be thin? Why did I spend so many hours of my youth daydreaming of being skinny? Because I equated being thin to being liked, to dating, to wearing cute clothes and being able to shop. Because the world taught me happiness and success are often linked to beauty and physical appearance, just as much if not more, than your talents and abilities. It was all superficial.

I would tell myself every day I'm going on a diet tomorrow. Tomorrow would be the start of a new me, and tomorrow never came.

Once I lose enough weight and once my hair gets long enough I'll be happy. Happy was always just over the fence of losing weight. Over the fence of being pretty enough. Happiness was always just a grasp away from me.

Then you lose weight and happiness still doesn't come. You lose weight and everything and nothing changes. A paradox. You must not have lost enough since you still aren't happy. You think once you get to a certain weight, you'll find happy. But happy isn't a number on a scale or a jean size, its internal which makes it harder but all the more necessary to obtain. You gain the weight back and hate yourself even more. It's a never ending cycle that hinges on the belief that as soon as I lose weight, I can start living. I spent so much time waiting to live that I missed life happening.

When I was a preteen, as part of a family trip, my dad took all of my brothers and me on a road trip to Jefferson City to visit our grandparents and then travel to Six Flags amusement park in St. Louis. I have honestly never been a big fan of amusement parks, especially roller coasters, but I go, ride a few rides and usually have a good time.

When we got to Six Flags, we conquered the park ride by ride, starting with the Batman rollercoaster. Towards the middle of the day we came to a rock climbing wall, an activity you must pay additional for and isn't included with the price of admission. All of my brothers and myself wanted a turn. My dad, surprisingly, paid for all of us to climb. When it was my turn I went to put on the harness and it didn't fit. I tugged but it wouldn't go up. I was mortified. Embarrassed. Sad. Disappointed. My dad took my turn instead, having already paid. I watched in sadness, tears stinging the back of my eyes, as he geared up and tackled the wall like a pro, climbing to the top and coming back down. I couldn't even fully enjoy the rest of the day— that moment ringing in the back of my head.

The next morning, my dad took me down to the lobby for the continental breakfast at our hotel. Just me, so we could talk. He knew the rock climbing fiasco affected me.

"Charell, do you know whenever you see a skinny girl you look down?"

I looked at him in disbelief, shrinking even further into myself. It was not only eye opening it was further humiliating as if not fitting the harness wasn't enough.

"No, I didn't know."

"Why do you think you do it?"

36

"I want to be skinny," I said. It was simple. I knew being fat was a curse and in my mind skinny was a prerequisite for beauty. I was far from beautiful but if I was skinny it would be a step in the right direction.

"Stop looking down. If you want to lose weight do what you need to do to lose weight," my dad said.

He made it seem so simple. What power did I have? I didn't buy groceries. I didn't have a gym membership. How could I be skinny?

"You're like me," he said. "Your body will adjust to what you do to it, and quickly. You work out and eat right your body will lose weight. You eat junk and do nothing you'll gain the weight back. You need to stop looking down and make changes."

Our talk continued in this same vein. His speech, good-hearted at nature, only compounded the fact that I felt unworthy, and now even my dad noticed. I still struggle with my beauty, constantly comparing myself to others and looking down when someone I thought was gorgeous was present. I've battled with being the designated ugly fat friend (DUFF) of the group my entire life, I mean really, look at my friends they are gorgeous. I felt like I was the odd woman out, like somehow I snuck into their crew and they allowed me to stay. Of course, that's not true, but that's how I saw it.

Since that trip to Six Flags, every time equipment or harnesses are involved in an activity I am sent right back to that place of insecurity. Summer 2015, I was 25 and attended my first young adult Christian retreat. Besides the amazing sermons, the retreat was on a campsite with a zipline and obstacle courses for us to take part in. I wanted to zipline, first and foremost. My friend Lauryn agreed to go zip lining with me so we got in line, beating the crowd. Though we beat the crowd, we were the last to go. *Why?* Because I couldn't get a harness to fit. I saw girls that looked to be about my size going so I wondered *why me? Again? Not again. I can't take it*. The girls working the zipline and my friend tried to pull the small harnesses up my body to no avail. It was sad, and I tried, unsuccessfully, not to mention my weight, but it's always there with me. I was feeling defeated and wanted to give up. As each person came down the line landing in the camp's lake I got sadder and sadder. They would remove their harness and I would hold it up to see if it was big enough and try to put it on. Finally, I got one that fit! My friend and I proceeded to the top of the line and propelled down, in what was my first zipline experience.

I have now not only zip lined, but I have done indoor rock climbing and a ropes course. The harness fit each time and I completed my goal of making it to the top and finishing the course. More so than reaching the top and the physical challenge was the success of having the harness go past my thighs over my hips and around my waist. Happiness was a harness. I had finally lived. I had lost some weight, that I'll admit, but more than that I was doing things I never thought possible.

As I was losing weight, naturally my body changed. I could workout longer without getting winded. My energy levels increased. But more than the physical health benefits one thing mattered the most:

I could cross my legs.

I could cross my freaking legs!

Someone who has been thin their entire life might not understand the joy that ran through my veins. I have been fat my entire life, always slightly pudgy, big-boned, chubby or whatever clever way was popular to say fat without actually saying the word fat.

As a young girl I was taught to cross my legs at the ankles and bring them under your chair, it was deemed the ladylike way to sit. However, as a young girl I thought it was so cool and sleek to cross your legs at the knee. It seemed like the most beautiful people did it and I wanted to. However, these thighs and gut would never allow for such a thing to occur. With weight loss I could finally cross my legs not at the ankles but over the knee. That was one of the sweetest tastes of victory I'd ever had.

***

There had come a point where I had lost over fifty pounds and with it I felt much more confident about myself, superficial and surface confidence. It only skimmed the surface. My confidence had never marinated, gotten deep in my bones and into my consciousness. What I mean is I needed outside affirmation to believe my worth.

No one tells you you can't lose weight and gain confidence. Confidence couldn't be found in crossing my legs or wearing a harness. Your mind doesn't change with your body. I tried to outrun my insecurities but I couldn't. I couldn't lose them away like my weight. And because my mental wasn't right I continued to gain and lose weight, continuing the cycle over and over again.

So much of my existence is defined by my weight, my pants size. I'm working to reverse that definition. To define myself. People would tell me, *"Girl if you lost some weight you would be a showstopper; it's really the only thing holding you back."* I'm learning that my body is not an apology. That the way I stand firm in my mind I should stand firm in my form. That I am allowed to take up space and not to shrink.

I try to recall these thoughts the moment the four boys insult me and it works briefly, I mean, I felt good when I left the house. I try to remember these thoughts every day when I encounter negativity- whether it's from someone else or my mind's creation. I try to remember the feeling that, Charell, you are growing and glowing in this world. You, my dear, reading this, are growing and glowing in this world.

I have yet to meet any person with no insecurity or a self-perceived flaw. Everyone, and especially women, that I've met has something they are unhappy with. Something that makes them insecure. But here's the secret: your insecurity is yours and no one else can see or know it unless you broadcast it. The very thing you hate nobody notices, it's true. I promise.

I've spent my whole life chasing beauty thinking once I'm beautiful, I will be happy. Missing the moments that make today and looking back with regret. When I stopped chasing beauty I was able to fully enjoy my life.

TABOO

The most powerful thing in the world
Is found between a woman's legs

In July 2016, the state of New York removed its "tampon tax,"
which no longer labeled menstrual products as luxury items.
Since the 1960s, the state had been taxing menstruation goods
while other medical goods were tax exempt. New York is one of
only five states that do not charge a tax.

I'll be blunt here: *why the hell are tampons being taxed?* I'll
even do one better, why aren't they free? It's not some freaking
privilege to bleed once a month. The only luxury is the day after
a period when I no longer have to wear a diaper and can resume
wearing my good drawers.

Becoming a woman is a bunch of bull.

I never even knew what a period was until it decided to show
up one day unannounced.

My period is not my girlfriend, it is an annoying ex-lover I
can't get rid of. Gone from my mind and my life, I can relax,
breathe again, and fit into my skinny jeans. Then my head hurts,
and my stomach cramps signaling a storm is brewing. He rushes
through causing nothing but turbulence, ruining my days,
nights, attitude, tastes and good underwear. The only comfort I
get from his steady return of beating my door down asking for

another chance is that it's necessary for the children I want to have in the far future. As I grew older and read more books, I saw that some girls really looked forward to their period, that first drop of blood meaning the world to them. I can't say the same for me. My entry into womanhood was unexpected and unwelcome.

I was ten, in the fifth grade and attending public school. My parents had decided to move us from the inner city schools to public school in the suburbs. We lived with our mom in the city but my dad had a home in the suburbs and we used his address since they had joint custody. That morning in my mom's home, I woke up slightly dazed, like always, and made the heavy sleep laden walk to the restroom outside of my bedroom. My eyes were barely open, I pulled my panties down and sat on the toilet. Something was wet, but I was nowhere near conscious enough yet for it to register. I opened my eyes and looked down to see not a spot of blood but dang near a pint of blood. My panties were completely drenched in red and you better believe that woke me up quickly. I was scared out of my mind.

"MOM! THERE IS BLOOD IN MY UNDERWEAR!" I screamed at the top of my lungs. I didn't move from that toilet until my mom came rushing. For all I knew I could be dying, and these were my last moments on earth. How sad that my last moments on earth would be on a bathroom toilet.

Mom explained that I started what was called a period. She cleaned me up and said, "*You're a woman now.*" She helped me to put on a pad and we rushed to finish getting ready to leave for school. She called the school nurse to inform her and request she talk to me about it since we were low on time and she couldn't afford to be late for work.

At school, the nurse, a kind, young, black woman, called me to her office. She explained what a sanitary napkin was, how to change it and said I was now a woman. There's that word again, woman. What does *I am a woman* mean? What the hell does blood coming out my private parts have to do with being a woman? I had no clue and only later would I piece it together. This evil red demon that was supposed to visit monthly meant I could have kids. *How do you have kids?* I still really did not understand, but I knew I could now, at age 10, have a kid. That was all the teaching I got. Mom had rushed to get us to school on time and the nurse simply broke down what a period was. There was no talk of birds and bees and I was still in too much shock to have questions, let alone one of substance that would bring clarity to what was happening. I discovered girls in my class had their period too. I felt better knowing I wasn't alone. They seemed so mature talking about it, a lot of them had expected it and were excited about it. I couldn't be excited about something I never even knew was possible. And the way it happened wasn't anything pretty to brag about either.

Seeing as my period started as a tsunami, it's no surprise it continued to wreak havoc on my life. Once a month for at least four years I was guaranteed two things- that I would leak through my clothes, requiring my dad to bring me a wardrobe change to school, and that I would have the worst cramps imaginable.

In the movie Sixteen Candles, one of Molly Ringwald's eighties classics, her sister Ginny, played by Blanche Baker, gets married. Unfortunately, she has her period on her wedding day and is doped up on painkillers. She passes out briefly before she walks down the aisle and stumbles down the entire aisle, but before she makes it to the altar she rests for a second on a pew. The scene is comical and though not as legendary as Jake waiting outside leaning on his red Porsche it was like watching my future. That could be me when I get married if I didn't plan accordingly.

Ginny is me. I am Ginny.

Hobbling from either the pain of cramps or the power of the medicine.

43

No joke, it was like the devil created PMS. Crippling cramps that made me sweat, puke and not do anything but lay down for the day. My pain would be so bad I would pray and make promises to God, *"God if You take this pain I promise I will be nice to my brothers and never disobey my Momma again."* You know how we do making promises we will not keep, but in the moment of pain you know you'll do whatever it takes to feel better. God and I were guaranteed to get real close at least once a month. If I hadn't talked to God regularly before you can be sure I was when I was cramping.

My mom handled my period well, as expected. She was a woman and apparently crippling cramps were genetic. She and my aunt both had it bad when they were young and even took to prescription medication to ease some of the pain.

My dad, on the other hand, did not handle having a little woman well. When I needed to get pads, he would drive me to the store, hand me ten dollars, and let me go in alone. You can imagine how many times I bought the wrong things. I was 10-years-old in a feminine care aisle and had not a clue what to get. I bought panty liners, super-size pads that were longer than my underwear, pads too short for my body, pads that didn't catch heavy flows. It was a disaster.

During one of my basketball team stints I had my period during practice. Per usual, my dad took me to the store, and I went in trying to decipher the hieroglyphics that are feminine hygiene products. Purple and pink bags and boxes surrounded me. *Light. Ultra. Thick. Heavy flow. Regular. Thin. Panty liner. Tampon. Super absorbent.* All these adjectives and nouns staring at me. I was lost and overwhelmed. The options were endless. I found a package that looked like it might work this time. It was a pad with a purple wrapper. The packaging read they were heavy flow, extra-large. Perfect, I bleed a lot and I'm extra-large. I had hit the pad jackpot, no more spotty underwear for this girl. I unpacked a few pads into my gym bag and we were off to practice.

I had to change my pad and went into the locker room adjacent to the gym. I pulled down my underwear and unwrapped the pad. It was humongous. I didn't even know anything could be that big. It was about the size of my forearm, thick with four wings. I placed it slowly in my panties trying to figure out how this would work. It was ridiculous, and now I would have to tell dad I bought the wrong thing and we have to go back to the store for more pads. I put the diaper on and went out to practice trying to be comfortable.

Besides my horrible pad shopping abilities, my dad instated a rule that wounded. I shared a bathroom with my five brothers and I wrapped my pad in the wrapper, as I had been taught, and threw it in the trash. My dad saw this and said to throw my pads away in my bedroom trash, not the bathroom so that others, i.e. him and my brothers, didn't have to see it. *Can you imagine how it embarrassing it is to have to walk from the bathroom with your pad in hand before you can throw it away and wash your hands?* For one week every month I felt like a stranger in my home, as if being a stranger to my body was not enough, and I hated it. It made me feel dirty. Wrong pads, pads in my bedroom trash, crippling cramps and a flow that could rival Niagara Falls all led to my intense hatred of Flo, or being on the rag as my grandpa Bobby would say.

Not only were my periods bad, but in the house we lived in with my mother there was a time we had no hot water. My mom would microwave big bowls of water and fill the tub for our baths. Sometimes we would use the same water for all of us. My mom's cycle would usually sync with mine or shortly follow it. She would shower in cold water if necessary. I would use the hot bath water last so my brothers wouldn't have to bathe in bloody water. I can honestly say my life has not been full of strife. I didn't have everything but I always had enough, but that was one time it was really bad for us. That house had several problems, hot water being one. My mom is a quiet warrior. She'll do whatever she has to for her kids and for that I am eternally grateful. She made my periods bearable.

I think my dad was really overwhelmed at the thought of his daughter becoming a woman. And even today he doesn't handle my feminine needs all that well. I do my best to keep that knowledge from him, asking to stop at a pharmacy and not telling what I need and wrapping the pad in the wrapper and toilet paper before sticking it in the wastebasket. I've never felt comfortable being on my period with my dad. It's not something I should have to hide and as a young girl, I'm sure having to hide or feeling like I had to hide it led to some embarrassment regarding what it means to be a woman. I was no longer like my brothers; I had this bleeding vagina that no one else in the house had. Life in the shadows seemed to continue.

My uterus was not my friend. As if my own body rebelling against me wasn't enough, the world outside was and continues to be unaccommodating. A woman's period is a taboo topic, at best it's briefly mentioned as *that time of the month* or ignored altogether unless the government and powers that be are trying to establish laws to control the uterus. Taking pride in something that caused me physical pain and seemingly family ostracizing took time. It was once a source of shame. Now, I don't whisper about it in embarrassment. I purchase pads, in the proper size and flow for me, and no I don't need it double bagged so the outside world can avoid seeing my purchase. I share stories of crippling cramps with friends and if needed I can be a resource or an empathetic shoulder. We're all in this bloody jungle together after all, right?

BUCKWHEAT

My hair is barbed wire
Keeping in my enslaved roots, ties me to my ancestors
Poking at European construct
Daring them to come into my territory
This land here is unconquerable

From barrettes to braids, to cornrows, to curls, wraps and everything else I've done most of it.

Greasing my scalp.

Hot comb on the stove.

My cousin braiding my hair so tight it hurt to smile.

Beads adorning my crown swinging with every head turn.

Ah, the memories. Memories that seem exclusive to black girls everywhere. For every black woman you meet there is likely a hair story, good ones and horror stories mixed into the overall narrative. We all have experienced our tresses being primped and styled. I am one of many who shares the memory and can easily recall the smell of a pomade, lotion or gel being applied to the hair. It was a part of growing up, like riding your bike or jumping rope.

My grandma Melanie told me she always had one gripe about my paternal great-grandmother. Apparently my great-grandmother took one look at me, her being of mixed heritage and no one able to pinpoint her lineage, and said, "*Whoa, that baby got some nappy hair.*" I had coarse hair like my dad and thick hair like my mother. I was nappy by nature, I came by it honestly, and apparently her "good hair" genes could not hold strong through the generations. This was the crown I was given and it would have to do.

When I was little, I wanted long silky hair — "white girl hair" I called it. I envied anyone who had long hair. Hair that touched your shoulders or cascaded down your back was the ideal image of beauty, at least that's what the world told me.

Instead, I had short, nappy hair.

In fourth grade, I lied about my hair. I had spent the entirety of my beloved Saturday at the beauty shop, like many a black girl. I was so excited to get something fun and new done to my hair. My hair was slicked up into a short weave ponytail. The stylist also added a few tracks of hair to the front of my head to create a cute, swooped bang. I loved it. I felt so pretty and couldn't wait to get to school on Monday to show everyone else how good I looked. I wrapped my hair carefully at night and slept with a stiff neck so as not to disrupt the style. When I went to school, I was standing in line with some girls from my class.

"Why'd you get weave?" one asked with her lips twisted and eyes raised.

"I don't know," I replied timidly. Her response was not what I wanted or expected.

"Yeah, that's weave," another chimed in with a condescending tone.

I instantly felt the need to defend myself or claim this style wasn't all weave. I had hair on my head, obviously, or the tracks wouldn't have anything to hold onto and the ponytail wouldn't be possible.

"This is weave of course," I said pointing to my ponytail. "But this is mine," I said gingerly patting my bang, the silky hairs of the track below my fingertips telling me I was a liar. I couldn't stand to have those girls think I was bald and didn't have any hair. They acquiesced, and we moved on to some other topic relevant to adolescent girls.

In middle school, my hair was somewhere between relaxed and natural and an entire disaster. My brothers and I were staying with my dad weekly while my mom took night classes to complete her undergraduate degree. My dad's fiancé Dionne, was great and helped to do my hair and show me styling options. She taught me how to roll my hair at night in curlers and that became my go-to style, I didn't know what to do any other way. Bad hair, teenage awkwardness, being overweight and crazy hormones led to many undesirable middle school moments, so many they could be a book all by themselves.

Sophomore year of college, in 2009, the same year *Good Hair* was released, I started relaxing my hair. Waiting months at a time to go home for the holidays wasn't cutting it and I was tired of looking like a ragamuffin. I decided I could do it and do it I did. Every four to six weeks I took to the creamy crack removing any kink or curl that dared ruin my straight hair.

Little did I know I was not doing such a good job. I didn't rinse out the relaxer completely and the back of my hair broke off. The bottom of my hair was nearly nonexistent, and I had failed to notice. When I did notice, after graduating college and returning home, I resumed seeing my beautician and worked to regain healthy hair. My usual roller wrap covered my lack of hair with no problem. However, updos and buns showed the world how sparse my hair was and my bright scalp shined through the wisps of hair. I would strategically wear headbands to cover my head and style over the missing hair. Despite the damage, relaxers were what I saw as my only hair care option.

Then I went natural, or rather natural came for me. I had just moved to New York and my last perm was two weeks prior so my tresses were still silky. However, slowly but surely, I transitioned. Part of my lack of reluctance to going natural was the culture of the city. There was an overwhelming feeling of self-expression and freedom I had experienced nowhere else (anywhere else being Missouri and my few trips out of state). Everyone walked to their own beat in the city and be damned to anyone who had something to say about it. And to be honest, going natural was cheap. I had no job and couldn't afford my bi-weekly maintenance appointments. I looked into finding a decent salon in the city and they were all expensive.

Missouri and my lifelong beautician had spoiled me, I had no more access to affordable wash and sets or relaxers. After my college fiasco, I knew self-relaxing wasn't for me and not worth the hassle. I decided I would not get my hair professionally done in the city and that I also would no longer do at-home perms. I had learned my lesson and natural was the only way to go for me at this point. I transitioned from April to December 2013. I had two go-to styles: braids and two-stranded twists into a halo around my head. These two styles and the occasional curly 'do kept my hair intact while I went relaxer free. I decided that when I went home for Christmas that year, I would have a stylist chop off my relaxed hair.

I went home and immediately booked a beautician to cut my hair. I am really surprised at how easily it went, even though I was sad, it wasn't as traumatic as some of my past haircuts. I was ready for the cut, it wasn't something I could run from, and eventually I would have to big-chop. Managing two different textures was a lot of work so the chop was as practical as it was emotional.

Now I had a small afro and there was no going back. My hair was all gone, and this was what I was left with. I had no choice but to embrace it and sure enough, I loved my natural hair. Even with bad hair days, I knew I would not be getting a perm anytime soon.

I have officially been natural for almost four years and it has definitely been a journey. To most black women hair is major and whether we like to admit it or not, many of us tie our hair to who we are, an intrinsic part of our identity. Even after my big chop, I had women tell me they could never cut their hair that short, and I had a decent amount of hair left on my head.

***

As much as people may love or hate Chris Rock's polarizing documentary *Good Hair,* it sparked a dialogue and brought attention to black hair. It challenged the status quo. *Why did we get relaxers?* It seemed as if relaxers were often a requirement, instead of another styling option, for many women. I honestly never thought of how odd it was to chemically alter the hair growing from my scalp to match what was already on my head, and so many other black women and girls didn't either. Perms were just what we did unless you looked like Chili from TLC with laid baby hairs. Relaxers were a part of self-care, of your maintenance routine, it was done subconsciously. However, once something is pointed out you become increasingly aware of it, in this case, it was our hair. I remember seeing the documentary in college with my friends. We were all excited to check it out at the local independent film house. We went one night and after leaving the theater and walking back to campus conversation, no doubt, ensued.

"Oh no, I am never giving up the creamy crack."

"Girl I need this. Have you seen my head?"

"Natural ain't for everybody."

We were on a roll that night with all of us agreeing we would not be going natural. I was vice president, if not the president, of the Black and Relaxed Fan Club. If my nappy roots were meant to be relaxed, what is natural? That's only for those pretty curly haired girls. Not me boo. All of us were beautiful shades of brown from light to chocolate with hair that ranged from short, to long and in-between, "good" and "bad." We were our own mini black girl coalition and unanimously we were all going to be relaxed.

Funny enough, now, all of my college friends are natural. Every single girl that walked the sidewalk that night cracking jokes on being natural and nappy headed are now beautifully natural and flourishing with hair healthier and longer than we had in college. It's interesting how things work out.

***

Gymnast Gabby Douglas was America's darling in 2012 and quickly became an object of critique during the 2016 Olympics. She could not win for losing— which she was far from a loser with three gold medals, successfully competing in two Olympic Games and making history in more ways than one. Gabby, as a 16-year-old teenager was critiqued because of her hair. The internet went ablaze during her first Olympics in 2012 criticizing her hair. The 2016 competition proved to be no different, though Gabby's hair had "improved," harsh judgments were still made. The thousands of critiques mostly came from black women. Gabby Douglas, like me and many other women, has a courser texture of hair that no amount of edge control and gel will keep slicked down when you're sweating and exerting energy. Despite all of Gabby's accomplishments, leave it up to internet trolls to focus on the insignificant: hair. Do a Google search for Gabby Douglas and "hair" is in the top three popular search terms that populate. She continued to be the target of ridicule and harsh judgment. The subject of hair in the black community is major, never grows old and is always at the forefront of many conversations. It's as if your appearance must be validated before you are. Gabby is busy and her hair is not, and should not, be the focus of conversation. She is flipping in the air, jumping from beams and defying gravity all while making it look easy. Gabby's hair meets gymnastic regulations and is practical- the most crucial part. Who has time to lay baby hairs while twisting in the air? The constant commentary on her hair is not only unnecessary, it's rude. The good news is that during the 2016 Olympics, the haters were being shut down swiftly. People were coming to the defense of Gabby and focusing on her talent, not her hair. Gabby was too busy taking over the world and snatching edges, so people needed to not worry about hers.

Even with the move to go natural, there is still division among black women, Gabby's story is just one example. It seems humans will always find a way to separate themselves; if it's not skin, then it's hair texture. There was a lot of debate in the online natural hair community regarding texture discrimination, there was an overwhelming fondness for baby hairs and silky curls, leaving out women with kinky and coarser hair textures. The world of YouTube tutorials overflowed with 3A/3B hair types. Interestingly enough the most criticism I receive about my hair is from other black women. Women openly critique my naps or kitchen, which believe me this 4C will never be slicked without the help of tension pulling hairstyles and edge pomade. My hair is not suited to easily slick down, it shrinks quickly and often, but some of my critics don't seem to comprehend that. It is *my* hair, however, some black women still comment on my tresses like they own claim to them or need my natural hair to appease their expectations. Black women can be unfairly and harshly over critical of each other, and the sources of why can be debated and researched further. I feel that as a group black women should be as unified as possible against the constant vilification the world throws us, instead of, at times, partaking in the breakdown of another black woman. Our hair and skin are under constant outside scrutiny and division among us can only aid in destruction.

A light-skin nappy hair girl or a dark-skinned gal with long flowing hair and everything in between, I'm ready for it all to be seen and glorified individually, not comparatively. We face enough external criticism, for example, wearing your hair in its natural state is seen as an act of rebellion. From the young girls in South Africa protesting their school for the right to wear their hair as it grows out of their scalp to people in corporate America who are told dreadlocks and afros aren't professional and deemed unkempt. With the federal court decision ruling that not hiring a person with dreadlocks is NOT discriminatory coming nearly simultaneously with Marc Jacobs cultural appropriation, his models paraded down the runway in faux locs for fashion week, it becomes increasingly important that our voices are heard and shared. It is a sad fact that when you Google professional hairstyles or the word dreadlocks both result in images of white people- a conundrum to say the least. The methods may vary but the message stays the same — black women and their features are often seen as commodities for the world but not for themselves.

I am often described as light-skinned with nappy hair- a funny juxtaposition for it goes against colorism and the Eurocentric values that are often lauded. The values that lead people to call Lupita Nyongo and Kelly Rowland beautiful- they are dark-skinned yet have slim facial features equated with European beauty. Angelina Jolie is called beautifully exotic- though you can throw a rock in my old neighborhood and hit a girl or boy with full lips; yet, simultaneously Viola Davis is called "less than classically beautiful" with her dark skin, coarse hair and full features. Even in the black community the desire to have fairer skin, slim features, and silky tresses runs rampant. My mom and her twin fit the often desired physical features of light skin, light eyes, and good hair. In fact, many in my family fit this narrative if not light-skin then it's good hair, and if they have coarser hair they are fair-skinned. It was the constant surrounding of these women, and men, in addition to media imagery that shaped my idea of what beautiful was.

It seemed the media showed no images of girls that looked like me. I was obsessed with fashion and would read multiple magazines a month to see what was popular, who was wearing what and how to dress. In most of my magazines there was little to no representation. Every month, I would eagerly open my magazine to catch up on the latest celebrity news and fashion. I would get to the hair section and sometimes would not see any black girls. If there was a black girl, she was usually light, mixed or racially ambiguous with long, curly hair. I could do nothing with the hair tips but look and yearn for hair like the models. I would flip further excited for the fashion stories and the style-on-a-budget features, knowing none of the items shown would ever be available in my size. When the magazines ventured to plus sized styles, the model was a size 12 with a flat stomach and an hourglass shape. No representation for me, yet I steadily consumed these images that were silently telling me I was wrong. That my skin was a tad too dark, my hair too short and too coarse, my body too big. If I wanted what the girls in the glossy had, I had to change and be like them.

I remember as a child thinking, *"At least I'm not dark."* It was one thing to be fat and nappy, but to be fat, black and nappy had to be a curse. I thought to myself, *"I barely made the cut,"* but I was glad I did. The world had taught a menacing lesson: to abhor my blackness.

The movie *Precious* starring Gabourey Sidibe focused on a fat, black and nappy teenager and her intrinsic and external struggles with an abusive mother, teenage pregnancy, and an HIV diagnosis. Throughout the movie, Precious dreams of having a "light-skinned boyfriend with real nice hair." I was Precious minus the abuse, babies, and overall gloomy storyline. I was Precious in that I was heavy and unhappy. I dreamed of a perfectly handsome, light-skinned man who would love me for myself too, or better yet, I would be skinny with long hair and he would love me skinny. The film showed what I came to expect, an overweight nappy black girl living an extremely unhappy life.

The entertainment world is changing and the diversity of narratives are increasing. In the Starz hit show *Survivor's Remorse,* one episode addressed colorism in the black community. The show follows a family who hit it big with the success of Cam Calloway, a young basketball star. His success led to moving the immediate family to his team town and chronicles their hilarious ups and downs with new money. In the episode titled "The Photo Shoot" Missy, played by the amazing Teyonah Parris, organized a photo shoot for Cam. The original model she chose was unavailable and was replaced by a model with light-skin and green eyes, the opposite of the original model choice. Missy arrives late, sees the change and immediately objects. She says, "Do you know what every dark-skin girl thinks when she sees only light-skin girls in magazines? They think their dark skin has made them invisible." In this short yet poignant scene Missy brings to light the history of colorism in the black community, touching on the paper bag test, and the damage that taking a stance can have on individuals. Missy made a relevant and much-needed point on displaying beauty and how the images we see dictate what we equate to success and more so our own personal self-worth.

As much as I loved the episode I still cringed. Parris is beautiful and looking at her I was very aware, and slightly envious, of that beauty. Her body is slim, yet curvaceous, her skin smooth and clear and her hair big and bouncy. I cringed at Parris's woe is me monologue because representation is more than skin tone. It is about size, ability, religion and more. Missy took a stance for brown women and I empathized with her desire for representation, even as someone who has been called light and undoubtedly leans towards the more inclusionary end of the black color spectrum. Though not light-skin with light eyes I had no issue seeing women of my skin-tone reflected, the pickings of black women in any media were slim and the ones featured were light, no doubt about that. The points of that episode were valid and necessary but there is still more to be done that I hope to see.

**

Now, there is a new black renaissance taking place. Young black girls are seeing themselves more and more, and when they do, it is affirming. If not in traditional media, it is through social media and other independent guerilla movements. A young girl can see herself in ways she never could before. They can see themselves reflected as beautiful, without exception, and hopefully they will avoid the immense amount of self-loathing and deprecation I faced. My hair is my crown. What was once something I could never fathom liking is now a sense of pride. Every coil, kink, and curl is beautifully mine.

Women of all shades and textures are going natural for various reasons and I couldn't be happier. Natural hair is everywhere. We are wearing afros, wigs, braids, locs, low cuts and more. There is so much diversity to see within the community. Diversity that our children will see and allow them to recognize themselves. Find themselves and hopefully see that your skin and hair don't define you but instead are a part of you as a unique being that the world needs and is blessed by your presence.

Oh, I admire the new generation of black girls, and am glad to be in their ranks. These initiatives are growing and becoming movements. From Black Girl Magic to Carefree Black Girl we are affirming our own beauty. And I am here for all of it: to witness it, contribute to it, revel in it, find inspiration in it, and love my blackness wholly, completely and unapologetically.

HOGWARTS

During high school, I was a smart student but not successful. I put too much pressure on myself, for I was in gifted classes with other highly intelligent students. We took our ACT - a college prerequisite exam and though I scored well above average; I didn't feel like it was enough. My classmates had nearly perfect scores. I figured, if I can't be the best just don't be at all, and for most of high school, I operated in that manner. I turned in work late and my grades suffered. The only class I excelled in was debate as it was my one passion in high school. Debate helped mold me. I learned to research, speak and develop my voice. Looking back, I have to ask God to bless my debate coach for all I put him through. Coach handled dealing with a know-it-all teenager like a pro. But aside from debate, I did the bare minimum in high school.

One night during my junior year, I called my dad and broke down. "*I'm not ready for college,*" I said. I had come up with the logical idea to go to community college and then transfer to a four-year institution. I had failed a couple math classes, my weakest subject, and was barely getting by in others. My dad told me I could do it, that I was smart and capable. "*You're going to college,*" he said. My dad has always been a straight shot with no chaser. He doesn't make his words sweet to digest, and I can always count on him to break things down into the simplest terms. He calmed me down and talked me through my breakdown. He worked in education and could help me fully understand what I needed to do to turn around my current situation. *What was my GPA?* Maybe a 2.0. *What did I need my GPA to be for college?* A minimum of 2.5. *What do I want to study?* Fashion, of course. He told me someone's daughter he knew went to a school in Columbia, Missouri called Stephens College. The school had a nationally known fashion program, and it was close to home. The other art schools I looked at were on the east and west coast and seemed worlds away, nearly impossible to reach and incomprehensible. I looked at the school's website and was hooked. Part of me wasn't ready to move far from home. I wanted to be close enough to come back quickly if my family needed me, but far enough away to gain independence. I believe part of the reason for this was I've always felt a certain amount of responsibility for my younger siblings, being a surrogate parent growing up. Either way, Stephens it was. After the call with my dad, I made a 180 degree change. I excelled, focused on doing my best and not becoming discouraged at others success. I mastered tunnel vision and learned to focus on myself, doing what I needed to be accepted into college. I was accepted at Stephens College and enrolled for fall 2008, I would be attending a four year institution after high school.

There's been a lot of discussion, and heated debate, recently regarding black college students finding acceptance at predominantly white institutions (PWI) versus attending a historically black college or university (HBCU). I chose the former and went even further left by attending a women's liberal arts college. The debate itself is rather annoying, as it is one of privilege, and the fact of the matter is we all have our degrees. At this stage in life, I am of the mind we should be focused on lifting each other and reaching back to help our brothers and sisters. Many of my family and friends have attended a variety of institutions, from HBCU to PWI to trade school, and we are all trying our hardest to be the best versions of ourselves to pursue our dreams. And most of us, though we attended different institutions, are still paying the same person for our loans–Sallie Mae, or Navient as she goes by now.

I hate when people ask me if I would do anything different. I feel it's an unfair question. Our life is a culmination of our experiences and choices and the consequences, good and bad, of those decisions. Without the steps you took before and the lessons learned your current position in life would be different. My choice to attend Stephens affected my life for the good and bad, particularly as a black woman. My friends and I often joked that it was Hogwarts, full of eccentric people you couldn't find anywhere else. Founded in 1833, Stephens transitioned from a two-year college to a full four-year institution specializing in the liberal arts. With the school's specialized programs such as fashion, theatre, dance and equestrian studies, there was no shortage of personalities. It was a world all of its own. *Looking back would I have done things differently?* I can say no. I am curious how life would have been, but I don't want to redo it. I have so many amazing women in my life because of Stephens. I believe God makes you walk a certain path to get you to your next point. I guarantee the experiences, good and bad, which I encountered at Stephens made me more aware, and were part of what led me to create Strong and Elite, and probably to even write this book.

The excitement of undergrad is one that cannot be replicated. With the campus buzzing and everyone eager to form new friendships, no one is a stranger and everyone is a potential friend. The first night there, after my mom and dad helped me move in, I laid in bed that night scared out of my mind. I thought, *"What did I get myself into?"* Here I am, sleeping in a room with a complete stranger and I have no idea how I will figure this college thing out. However, over the next four years, I did, and better than I expected. I found my groove and excelled at my studies and my social life, having fun but never forgetting I came to get that degree. At such a small school, I became very good friends with the women on my dorm floor and the other black students on campus. And at a school with under 1,500 students even if you weren't friends, you knew who every other black girl was. I was in a tight clique and we had our fair share of drama, like everyone else.

Freshman year our clique was solidified after a night of partying got a little too out of hand. After sweating out our relaxers at that weekend's best party we climbed into our cars and headed back to the dorms. Four of my friends lived in a hallway to themselves so it was our main meetup point. My best friend Monica's boyfriend was in town and some of my other friends invited a few guys we had met previously at the party back to the dorm. We were all loud, happy and having a good time. As the guys filed into the hall, they were obnoxiously vulgar, seeming to stake a claim to a territory that was not theirs. My friend's boyfriend stepped into the hall to see what the commotion was about, as they were getting ready to sleep, and the four guys replied with a smart comment and jumped as if they were to hit him. All of this happened in probably five seconds but it seemed to move in slow motion. Monica and I hopped into action without thinking and our friend Ebony was ready to fight. These were four big guys who could easily hurt us, but I have never had a fear of someone putting their hands on me, I have an amazing amount of faith that I am safe. We all raised our hands and moved them toward the door.

All of our voices mixed to create a dangerous howl.

"Back the fuck up."

"Move ya ass!"

"Get out!"

"There's the door."

Our cussing out and directions were non-stop as we slowly pushed the guys to the door. But even once they were at the door they didn't want to leave. Our dorms had two sets of doors, and they were not outside yet, where it required a key to get in. As my friend Renee jumped ready to fight we were in the lobby gaining attention from the girls there watching a movie. But everyone was on our side, the guys had to go, and if needed security would be there in minutes. We managed to get them out and after had a million laughs about the night. That night was the first of many, but it secured one thing, that we all had each other's back. We spent college laughing together, studying together, even cooking Sunday dinners. To this day, though I'm not as close to all the girls anymore, we still keep in touch. We share a ton of memories from our four years at our own version of Hogwarts.

Within my core group emerged a threesome, Hilary, Monica and me. The three of us were a unit, always going out and studying together since we had the same major. We decided our junior year to take a real spring break trip. Real meaning the typical college student spring break with lots of partying and drinking near sand and surf. We went to Panama City Beach (PCB) in Florida, my first trip. After a series of crazy plan changes and weather delays we landed in PCB ready to party. We did more than just party though; we were bona fide tourists. We swam with dolphins, went parasailing, jet skied and rode a banana boat. Every day was an adventure, and every night was a party.

We lived young and a little reckless during our trip. Our hotel was not near the beach and we relied on taxis to take us back and forth. However, we were tired of spending our money and at a fast food restaurant we met two guys with a car. They were about our age and locals to the area. We decided to save money and ride with them to the beach. We knew nothing about these guys except their names, but we had no fear and no cares.

63

But just in case we needed to open the door and roll out, Hilary, Monica and I sat alert in the back seat. As we rode we learned about the guys and what it was like living in Panama City Beach. Somewhere along the drive, the passenger felt very comfortable and told us about a sore on his foot. I sat directly behind him, and thankfully could not see, but Monica and Hilary got a full view as he lifted his foot and tried to pop whatever puss filled crater had inhabited his foot. My friends were on the verge of throwing up and I was horrified at his commentary narrating his actions. We got out of the car so fast when we reached the beach I don't think it fully stopped. We were all disgusted, but it could have gone wrong in many other ways, but that's what happens when you ride in cars with boys who are strangers.

I went to college on a mission: to get good grades, get a degree and get a job. In that order. High school had taught me I didn't have to be the best to be my best. There were other collegiate-focused activities I wanted to do, such as join a black sorority and travel abroad, but other than that there was nothing else that demanded my attention. Anything beyond that was a bonus. I got my degree and graduated with honors and other accolades, I had found my stride. I did not join a sorority, the organization I had wanted was not active, and could not study abroad due to financial challenges. I funded my education myself, with scholarships through my hard work, financial aid, and personal student loans. To study abroad, Stephens had a policy that boiled down to paying double the tuition, tuition for the school abroad and tuition for Stephens. I kicked, crawled and scratched to pay for it or change the policy, going so far as to meet with the school president. I had no luck and sadly had to watch my dream to study abroad die. That definitely left a bitter taste in mouth and it would be dishonest to portray it any other way. To feel like the school would in no way help, was heartbreaking. I was a great student and active on campus yet I couldn't do the one thing I really wanted to.

Though undergrad was full of hilarious moments with friends and personal and academic achievements there were downsides and disappointments. While enrolled my advocacy for minority awareness rose and so did my advocacy for black people specifically. I was still in Missouri, my home state, so I was no stranger to racial divides, however they became more pronounced and I became a target.

Being yelled at from a stranger sucks. Drive-by screams were common on nights in downtown Columbia, Missouri, where my campus was located. People would roll down their windows and scream or cheer in a drunken stupor, from pure joy or ignorance it always varied. It was usually from drunk white fraternity boys yelling *"nigger!"* or *"woohoo!"* at the top of their lungs because obviously black people are happy and partying at the trumped up rap music blasting from their speakers as they drive by. The drive-by screams, we were all used to in some form or another. It's no fun but when the incidents happen closer to home they hit, and hit me they did, hard.

Math has always been my weakest subject. I hate it just as much as I'm sure as it hates me for always ruining its finiteness with my errors. Midterm time at any college or university is stressful. It was for me. I was in my groove at Stephens and was determined to keep my GPA up, I wanted an "A" in everything but for a math class I would gladly take a "B" and leave with a smile on my face. As part of my major requirements I had to take statistics. I say requirement because only me having to be there would justify my presence in any math class after high school. I was struggling in the class. I was getting low scores on tests and quizzes, and my homework was usually full of errors. To top it off my teacher was also my academic advisor. I was very self-sufficient so my advisor was really only the in between to sign off on my planned course schedule, I didn't seek actual advising sessions from her.

As we entered the second half of the semester our teacher

was showing us our current standing in the class. Every eager student stayed and lined up to see where they were, turns out I wasn't the only one who loathed statistics and was struggling. I stood joking with my classmates as we continued to near the front of the line discussing other classes and our plans for the weekend.

The girl in front of me was now talking to the professor. She had a "C" and the teacher promptly said, "Don't worry you can still get an 'A.'" The girl in front of me was white with long blonde hair and blue eyes. This was not the first student with a lower grade that I saw the teacher comfort and encourage that day.

I was next. She looked at her notebook then back at me and told me I had a 'B-.' I was ecstatic. I was doing much better than I thought and it showed on my face. "Now don't get excited," the teacher quickly said, "you have a lot to do to get to the 'A' you want."

My mouth clamped shut immediately and my face screwed up. "I will get my 'A,'"I said curtly and left the class. I finished with a 'B,' which I worked my butt off for. . .

Prejudice and racism isn't always overt. It's subtle. It's woven into the tapestry of the American conscience and her simple rebuttal of my grades was all I needed. I noticed immediately and was taken aback. All the other students were reaffirmed, yet I was told I had a lot to do, one of the only brown students in the classroom. I believe it was that moment my slumber ebbed.

Do I think my professor intentionally meant to hurt me? No, but that doesn't nullify how she made me feel and what her actions meant.

Boy, did a sleeping giant wake up.

I could handle a teacher doubting me, the world is full of that, the constant battle of showing someone else what you are capable of. She didn't faze me. However, the next thing that happened my junior year hit closer to home.

One night when returning from a party I found someone had written on the dry erase board I left outside of my door. Boards are common practice on campus and I put mine outside my door in case my friends stopped by while I was out. That night I found my sign with negative comments written on it, the main one read:

Obama is a stupid nigger and a monkey.

Not that the sign was written on, it was the nature of the content that was bothering, I felt it was a direct target at my blackness. My dorm room floor was out of the way in a far off hallway you only entered if you lived on the floor. Besides that, I was the only black girl living on the floor and no one else had encountered any issues.

I felt targeted but more than that I felt unsafe, unwanted and was quickly reminded that your blackness doesn't make you exempt from hate. I took it to the Dean of Student Affairs and she handled it well. She allowed me to move rooms with no additional cost and filed an investigation report with campus security. I was honestly so humiliated I didn't want to make it public but I shared it with my friends on campus who were instantly, and rightly so, infuriated.

Despite the negative aspects, there was an abundance of positivity. One of my closest mentors is a Stephens alum and so are some of my closest friends. I can honestly look back without much chagrin and for that I am grateful.

At the end of my time there I was ready to leave, after four years every college student is ready to be an adult, we think. I met many remarkable women during my time there. I had great teachers, who still support me, and met some of my best friends. There is something to be said for the Stephens network, there is an unexplainable sisterhood you have with women who went there, we call ourselves Susies, no matter what year. You are instantly connected, and nine times out of ten you will find a way to help each other. When building my website my Stephens classmates, and even younger and older alumni, all had a hand in helping me realize my vision—and they volunteered their services quickly with no hesitation. I realize, that as always in life, God placed me exactly where I needed to be. I needed to refocus on being studious, successful and grow into a woman. Attending any other school I'm sure I would have succumbed to pressure to fit in and appeal to others. I had none of that pressure at Stephens. It truly was a community where any and every one could find a niche.

Though my school was small, it was a great experience and I can never take it back. There is nothing like undergrad. Even though I wasn't close to some of my peers in college, when we moved to NYC we sought each other out, just to have a support system and help in any way possible. You don't have to be friends, but being a Susie is a requirement. Through my time in NYC, I have created a solid support system of women. Whether I speak to them daily or once every few months the love is always there. There really is no other way to describe it than a sisterhood, a bond. And I must admit that the bond I have with my fellow African-American Susies may be stronger as we have the same shared experiences of being a minority at Stephens College. There are just experiences and issues that our white counterparts cannot relate to. So many women from my college have had a hand in helping me and my success, and I couldn't imagine life without them. I really went to school with great women and the world better watch out for us.

College is for exploration and fun. For making a ton of mistakes. Making friends and taking risks, doing things you may not be proud of but make a great story. It's when you encounter some of your toughest challenges and find you can solve your own problems, be your own hero. And if you do it right you'll leave with much more than just a degree.

LOVE, HAPPINESS AND ALL THAT OTHER -ISH

At a very early age, I decided subconsciously I didn't want to have kids outside of marriage, this was before I knew what sex or reproduction was. Watching my parents I learned what difficulties doing so would have. I knew I only wanted to have kids with my husband and that I wanted to be the only one with his children. I love my parents, and they have so much history I really can't comprehend all the nuances of their relationship. I've always been perceptive and very introspective, so in watching my parents and the complexities of their relationship, little Relly determined that she didn't want the same complexities in her life, and she would do all she could to avoid it. My parents were growing the same as me. From teens to adults they were struggling with normal young adult issues and insecurities with the bonus of a baby. Going to school, working multiple jobs and providing for their firstborn was difficult and as my family grew, so did the challenges. I had to grow and learn to see from their perspective, but that only came with time. As a child, my observation led to the following conclusion:

I don't know what I want but I know I don't want this.

***

My momma and daddy met when they were teenagers. My uncle Rick was dating my mom's friend and gave my dad's number to my mother. They then talked on the phone for at least four months before they met in person. When they first met, my mom walked to his house after school one day.

After their first meeting it was my dad who traveled. My daddy would run after track practice, or ride his bike, to meet my momma and hang out at her home. The family still jokes about his short track shorts- you know the ones from the eighties showing lots of thigh and leaving little to the imagination. That was the beginning of over a decade long infatuation and on-again, off-again relationship between my parents.

It was during these visits that their relationship blossomed. As they grew older so did their relationship moving from crush to love to single to love to single to parents. They grew together through middle school and high school going through the usual break- up and make-up that teenagers do, but this would end up being a lifelong relationship.

My mom had just graduated high school and before she could get a good grip on life and what she wanted to do, she was pregnant with someone else's life to consider—mine.

She waited a while to tell her parents. But even without her telling them they knew. My grandpa insisted that she was pregnant while my grandmother was in denial. Never mind that one of my grandma's closest friends, Uncle Risto, who was an apostle and a strong man of the Christian faith, had called her to tell he had dreamed of fish, and every black person knows fish means there's a baby in the midst.

My mother, a child herself, was committed to bringing this child in the world. She called my dad to tell him the news while he was away at boot camp for the Marines.

"Darrell, I'm pregnant," she said.

"What are you going to do?" he asked. The first thing that usually pops out of man's mouth. Daddy tells me this story all the time.

"I'm keeping it," she answered.

This phone call changed the trajectory of both of their lives. She was having a baby and their lives would be forever altered. They would be parents.

***

As a child, I watched and watched and watched. Melanie would always say, *"Charell ain't missed nothing. She's over there sucking her thumb and twirling her hair, but don't think she's not paying attention."*

My grandmother loved to share the story of when my parents were planning to get married. I had to be about four or five as it was before the twins were born. Apparently, my parents had planned to marry at the courthouse. My grandmother, mom and I were shopping for outfits for my mom, my brother and me. While in the store my grandmother says, and she'll never forget, that I pulled my thumb out of my mouth looked up at my mom and said, *"I don't know why you're buying all this stuff. My daddy ain't going to marry you,"* and continued sucking my thumb. My mother fumed and my grandmother had to stop her from whooping me while biting back her laughter.

People don't want the truth they want confirmation. The truth, as freeing as it can be, can also break hearts, ends worlds and force confrontation. Toddler Relly was giving no confirmation, only the truth served cold.

The story has always stuck out to me for several reasons.

One, I have always been an observer and intuitive. As a child, I was able to watch and get all the answers I needed without ever opening my mouth. I would think to myself, *my family don't say much to me but their actions tell me everything I need to know. Momma and Daddy don't agree on stuff. They don't seem too happy and things always seem hard for us. What do grownups have to talk about anyway? I know I'm 'sposed to stay out of their business so I don't say nothing. But I watch.* I observed and I drew conclusions, a contemplative child is not to be overlooked.

Two, my honesty in that moment. They do say out of the mouths of babes comes the truth.

Three, at some point my parents actually planned to marry, wow. My daddy married? At 25 years old? *Nope, no sir, it wasn't happening.* I like to think my daddy was a ladies man. What else could explain all of us kids by multiple women? He had to be something special, right? I mean I've never been in love, just a heavy dose of infatuation, but I can't imagine placing myself in a position to be a single-mother—the title I want first is wife.

Daddy has brown skin and a bald head, been that way for as long as I can remember. He's tall with brown eyes and walks slightly pigeon toed- even Darrell Jr. got that walk, one leg slightly off with the toe pushed in a little too much. If my daddy's looks weren't enough, he's funny. No really, he's funny. He has a joke for everything, and in another life, I could easily see him being a comedian. So he's funny, good looking, oh and smart. He was a first generation college student and after many starts and stops; he got his college degree and then another one and then his doctorate, but he didn't then. Even as a kid I was proud, didn't know what a degree was or what it meant but I knew it was important. Somewhere between all those degrees and starts and stops in school, there were more kids.

I was the first, Daddy was in basic training when I was born. After me, he knew he needed to go to school to give his kid a better life. Shortly after me came Darrell, we are almost Irish-twins. Darrell came in this world fighting—his little body was sick and barely made it. Momma and Daddy were so worried about him and his care demanded so much attention I was often with my grandparents. After Darrell came E'saias, but he has a different mom from us. Then came Preston, who also has his own mother, then the twins, from my momma. The twins were a major moment; not only was momma pregnant, but she was popping out two, a tradition that seems to hold strong on her side of the family. We were a gang of kids enjoying everything the nineties offered.

I don't have half-siblings- I have brothers, and now a sister. I love and respect not just my siblings but their mothers. Daddy made that clear. He raised us that way, and I have always been one to pick up on the values my parents wanted to instill in me.

Sure enough, there was no wedding. Instead my mom, brother and I took family pictures in the outfits that were supposed to be worn to the wedding. They look like Easter pictures: my brother in his vest and tie and me with my dress and hat. The pictures are nice. My mother was probably heart broken. My mother has never been married. My father was married, for a short stint. I am not a person who has ever pined for her parents to be together; it was never an option for me. They were my parents, and they were not together, so I accepted it as fact and had no issues with it. It was my normal. I couldn't comprehend kids who struggled with their parents' divorce or fathom having your mom and dad in the same house all the time, it was foreign. My parents have always shown me unconditional love and support, and I didn't need to see them married to receive it.

***

In addition to my parents dysfunctional relationship every single one of my grandparents has been married twice. My grandfather Bobby is not my biological grandfather. My papa Joe is not my biological grandfather either. Instead, on both my mother and father's side of the family my grandparents found that their second marriage was the successful one for a multitude of reasons.

My father's mother, Linda, and his dad, were divorced as long as I can remember and both remarried. My grandma Linda was in a toxic marriage. My grandfather was unfaithful and often undependable as a husband and father. After many transgressions she reached her breaking point. She was tired.

My grandpa has since grown, however the scars still linger for my dad and uncles. I was alive when my grandma met Joe and was a flower girl in their wedding. She had found the man she wanted to be with and would aid in her life walk.

Melanie was also divorced, and her second marriage was to my grandpa Bobby. I never even met my biological grandfather until I was 17 and haven't seen him since. I have a grandfather, his name is Bobby. My grandmother also loved to tell this story of my childhood perception as I asked her one day, *"Grandma you've been married before haven't you?"* Someway, somehow I had pieced together the fact that Bobby wasn't her first husband. He is the only grandpa I know and has shared so much with me I never considered him not my grandpa. "Bobby" was my first word. Seriously. Not Momma. Not Daddy. Not even Grandma. *Bobby.* I think it was Bobby instead of grandpa because as a baby I was often with my grandma and grandpa and she called him by his first name. Whatever the reason, I started a trend. All the grandkids called him Bobby. It was what we did. Before Bobby though, my grandmother was in a marriage that brought only problems. The father of her three children had proven himself to not only be a poor husband, but a bad father. He was unfaithful, did not contribute to the household or take an active role in his children's lives. She tried to stay married but realized staying would only do more harm than good. She used all her strength to leave and care for her children by herself. It was difficult, but it was necessary. Melanie worked multiple jobs to provide for her children and after several dating mishaps became careful about the men she introduced into her children's life. Before she married Bobby and allowed him into her and her children's world, he had to be approved by my mom and her sisters. Bobby was diligent in his pursuit and showed not only love to my grandmother but to her children. He was not perfect, but he was perfect for her.

***

Winter 2014 everyone was home for the holidays. My new niece was celebrating her first Christmas and my dad brought my brothers, my sister, my niece and her mom and me to visit my grandmother.

We were all sitting in the living room catching up fawning over my beautiful niece and talking about life. The topic of my dating life arose, they look at me and see a young, beautiful girl living in NYC who should be dating. By my age, a lot of young adults in the Midwest are seriously dating, engaged, married or married with children. This question isn't unexpected but it is exhausting. In my twenty plus years of life the answer has always been the same, "No, I am not dating."

That day I distinctly remember my grandma Linda telling me, "*Charell make sure you marry a man that loves you more than you love him.*" She said this in front of my papa, her second husband; my dad, her son; and my brothers, her grandchildren. It was at that moment I realized how much of a boss my grandmother was. If that isn't OG status, I don't know what is. She made it very clear I was to never be a doormat for a man's love but the center piece. To this day I remember her advice, I never want to be a man's footstool by loving too much, we need to be equal in our love and I would be on board for him to love me more.

***

From my parents I learned what I didn't want. I established my personal relationship requirements early and that has saved me many tears, saved me from many problems.

Melanie and Linda taught me that a relationship has no boundaries. That you define your role. That marriage is a union and should be acted as such. That you and your partner fill each other's short-comings. When those criteria are not met you are not only allowed, but obligated to leave.

My grandmothers were in unhappy marriages that led to divorce. For individual reasons they each struggled and suffered from loving and being with a man that can be destructive to not only your existence but to your children's existence. There comes a point when it will end, it's up to you if it will be voluntary or not. You can love and leave if he's no good. Melanie taught me that. Linda taught me that. My grandmothers taught me that.

Family is convoluted and complicated and messy, but it is full of love. Love grounds us and keeps us knit together. Through half-siblings and divorces and almost marriages and step-grandparents love always lingered. Love of self and for their children led my grandmothers to leave unhappy marriages. Love is the root of this tree. And love, happiness and all that other -ish is not only what I want, but what I require.

NOBODY KNEW

I keep my struggles and horrors locked inside
Which is why I struggle to write
Afraid of what will happen
When my truth comes to the light

I don't know when it started but I know it seems like it's always been a part of my life. One of those skeletons in the closet you want no one to know about. A dirty little secret. No, really, it was dirty, and it was my secret. From childhood or somewhere along the way I was exposed to sex, without fully comprehending what it was. As I entered my teenage years, I began watching pornography. A lot of it. I would sneak to watch it on HBO or on the computer when the dial-up cooperated. It consumed me. I had decided to wait for sex until marriage so I felt watching pornography was justified.

As I grew older and entered adulthood I watched it less, but when I was lustful or craving love, I filled those desires with porn. I would watch try to feel something good and then after feel completely disgusted. Unable to look at myself. Unable to forgive myself. I would pray to God to forgive me and promise to never do it again. Months later I would succumb to the temptation again. I was slightly consoled as I got older learning that most everyone watched porn by themselves or with their partner. I thought knowing it was a common occurrence would help assuage my guilt, but it didn't. I knew it was wrong, at least for me anyway.

Pornography led me to lust. Lust is a sin, and I was guilty of it. Through my actions, I wasn't keeping my body holy:

> *Flee from sexual immorality. Every other sin a person commits is outside the body, but the sexually immoral person sins against his own body. Or do you not know that your body is a temple of the Holy Spirt within you, whom you have from God? You are not your own, for you were bought with a price. So glorify God in your body.*
>
> 1 Corinthians 6:18-20 (ESV)

Before my mind could comprehend the sin, my spirit notified me I was wrong; that was the source of the guilt, and the guilt lingered.

The temptation seemed to be ever present. It would arise at the most annoying times, even enter my dreams, to a point where I could no longer ignore it. Sporadically, I would have urges and give in, however instead of hours it would be mere minutes or seconds before I turned off the porn. I told myself some progress was better than none.

I felt like a hypocrite. I was the good girl who went to church and was generally well-behaved. I was the girl who didn't have sex and was considered sweet and innocent, but here I was with this dirty secret that held itself over me. I would often have prayers where I degraded myself saying:

> *I am not worthy*
> *I am so sorry*
> *I am so pathetic*
> *I am so tired*
> *Of pretending to be strong*
> *Why me*
> *I can't even be mad at anybody*

Which makes it even worse
No one to blame but myself
I am so sorry Jesus
Oh God
Please
Please
Don't hold it against me God
I'm sorry

Praying and pleading with tears and a guilty spirit weighing heavily on me.

Summer of 2015 I took my first adult retreat. I grew up in church and had attended camp every year from about second grade to senior year of high school. It was at church camp I got saved and gave my life to Christ. It was there I forged bonds with church family, had fun with my best friends, ate s'mores for the first time, and got into water gun fights. The retreat, hosted by a Brooklyn based church's young adult ministry, was really intriguing. I had been regularly attending their young adult services for over a year and the promotional video for the retreat showed a huge lake and lots of praise and worship. I knew I had to go! My childhood church camp experience, with cabins and a lake, was calling. It was a chance to experience something new while also being thankful for my old memories. I didn't know what to expect, but I knew God would move.

The retreat was everything I wanted and more. I went zip lining and jumped from trees. I met amazing people. But more than that I heard God clearly, connected and grew in my spirit to a new level.

There were daily sermons where we turned-up for God, dancing and cheering and jamming to music all in the name of Jesus. Nothing was boring about praising God. There were guitars and drums and flashing lights, it was like a club, except we partied for Jesus.

While at the retreat I had a breakthrough. One night we were

79

praising after the sermon, the room was filled with the spirit and the worship team led us. I was praising and rejoicing and the worship leader spoke softly, *"Nobody knew but God. You are forgiven."* And it hit me. I screamed out *"nobody knew!"* and broke down crying right there, I sat down and just lived in the moment that a huge weight was lifted. All of my promiscuity and bad deeds, no matter how small or big they seemed were no match for God. I was free from it all. I knew mentally that God had forgiven me but I hadn't accepted that forgiveness in my heart and forgiven myself. God told me the chains were broken, I am no longer captive to those temptations.

That night my cabin mates and I gathered and talked about what we had experienced so far during the retreat. My friend Lauryn mentioned when I said *"nobody knew"* and it became our joke. Then, I had flung my arms high and screamed out in release, now, it was fun and hilarious and we could commune in happiness together. No one knew what my deliverance had been from but I shared that I was free and it was amazing.

My chains were gone. I learned and accepted that I can be free from anything. It is possible to be saved and not be free, and when that happens you are a prisoner, often of your own creation. Now I know I am no longer captive to my sins, I may feel guilty but I remember that God calls and qualifies. He's forgiven me long ago, and He's forgotten, so I need to do the same. My past sins will not be held against me.

Though I was free. I knew temptation would still come, but now I knew I had the power not to succumb. God would always give me a way out:

> The temptations in your life are no different from what others experience. And God is faithful. He will not allow the temptation to be more than you can stand. When you are tempted, he will show you a way out so that you can endure.
> 1 Corinthians 10:13 (NLT)

Now, unlike the past when I would ignore a way out of my temptation, I would purposely seek it out.

Sometimes I have been tempted to get on the internet and instead my phone will ring or I'll get an email that needs answering. I can ignore them or see them for what they are, an escape for me to avoid temptation and pass the time until the temptation subsides. I can't say I immediately made the change, I backtracked. Making the best choice isn't always easy, but the choice is always there.

Your personal demons and sins may not be mine, but know we do ourselves no justice hating and refusing to forgive ourselves. God forgives and forgets if we confess with our mouths and believe in our hearts.

God forgives, it is written in His word, over and over and over. He knows we are not perfect, that we all fail and that all sin is equal. There is no hierarchy of right and wrong in the Kingdom. Unlike humans, God forgives *and* forgets, I can't stress that point enough.

God pulled me out of sin I kept clinging to. That is the paradox for me, and many others, we hold on to the very thing we know eats at us, which tears us down brick by brick and weakens our foundation. We know it's bad but can't stop. Yet, no matter what, God still loves us and never let's go. There is no place too dark or too deep that His love and light cannot reach. I found it harder to forgive myself for my sins than it was for God to forgive me.

What makes God so good is that though I am so undeserving and unworthy, He still unselfishly gives me His love and forgiveness. That's what weighs me down most is that I sin against someone whose love is pure and unconditional.

Nobody knows what we personally struggle with daily, but God does, and He is the most important one. I had to take it to Him and be willing to release it fully in order to find a breakthrough. Your blessing is on the other side of your breakthrough.

STEPPING OUTSIDE OF MYSELF

She was grieving. She was desperate for attention. She was all of those things and more. All of those things and more can prime a girl to make bad decisions. She needed some semblance of control.

Black girl in NYC can't be just a black girl. No, she's not Dominican. No she's not Haitian. Where are you from? Here. So you are Spanish? No, here meaning the United States. From nowhere exotic. No island. No distant land. She's black. Regular black. She emphasizes regular. Maybe then they'll understand she's just a black girl.

She's everything and nothing. From everywhere and nowhere. And nothing and nowhere blends in. Tries to make home outside of herself.

She encounters a boy parading as a man. She relates as she's been wearing the costume woman for far too long and it's still uncomfortable. She would tell you more about him but it's irrelevant. The story isn't about him it's about her.

He spots her in the bodega. Watches her leave and makes his move. She doesn't understand at first. Why is he talking to her and what is he saying? He says, *you're beautiful* and asks for her number. He pulls out a flip phone.

Flip phone. Red flag. She ignores this and takes his number instead. She tells herself she won't call. She does. Again he tells her she's beautiful. She can't compliment him because she doesn't find him attractive, just available. Red flag number two.

He's blunt and his intentions are clear. *I want to taste you* he says during their first call. Red flag. She ignores. He sells weeds for a living. Red flag. She ignores. So many red flags keep rising and she pushes them to the side. She tries to shut her brain off, she wants to be a girl who only feels doesn't think. At least for a little while.

He says that she's fresh. That he can teach her. Guys like him don't encounter many virgins. But girls like her encounter many men who want to be first. Flag on the play.

She sees them all red and waving and blaring. Did she care? No. Internal brokenness contributes easily to falling. The things a girl will do for attention. She spent years praying for someone to notice. Leaped at the chance to be wanted, for however brief and superficial it might be.

He tells her she's sexy and she smiles inside. She doesn't have to dig for compliments, he gives them freely. She takes them willingly, devouring them like she's been starving. No meal this good has come her way in years.

She wants to feel wanted, for a fleeting moment at least. He lets her feel this.

Two days is all it takes for him to make a move. He weasels his way into her building but her brain turns on. He cannot enter her apartment. They stop on the stairs, between floors, she feels likes she's always in between something- past and future, decisions or something else, always straddling a nerve-wracking middle.

He kissed her tasting of smoke. She was repulsed and moved her head. He took it is an open invitation to her neck. He moves her to the wall and works his way down her body. He lifts her shirt. Takes breast to mouth and sucks. He's happy, while she is just there.

He pulls out his penis, hard from the mere thought of her or maybe it's just at the thought of another conquest. He thinks he'll leave with what he came for, which is her, of course. He wants her mouth on it, she refuses. She is desperate but her desperation appears to have a limit. She has allowed her brain to turn on for she is not desperate enough to contract disease and defile herself that way, giving head in a hallway to a stranger, quite yet. She places her hand on it and slowly moves it up and down. She doesn't like it and stops. He uses his own hand instead, what she won't do he can.

With one hand he puts his hands down her pants. She's completely dry as he explore her body. A desert that hasn't seen rain years. She was uncomfortable. It hurt. She wanted to stop, but she got herself in this situation. She stood there against the wall waiting for him to get what he needed, her, as much as she would and could give at that moment. An unsynchronized dance, painful to watch and even worse to be part of.

Standing there hoping it will end. Thinking how did she end up here? He ejaculates, a stream of white landing on the steps below their feet. She couldn't speak. What had she done? She was ashamed. Mortified. How did it get out of control? It didn't even feel good.

Why runs through her mind on endless loops. She feels dirty. She is embarrassed. She knows better. A girl searching outside herself for fulfillment makes these kind of mistakes.

My body is sore but it will recover fine. It's my mind and spirit I'm worried about.

SINGLE BLACK FEMALE

He kissed me.

Robert.

He kissed me.

In the coat closet of my first grade classroom I had my first kiss. But it wasn't really *my* first kiss. We were all getting ready, grabbing our bags and coats from our cubbies and the coat closet before we moved to our designated after-school care room down the hall at my elementary school. As I walked into the coat closet Robert was kissing one of my friends, Shayla. I opened my mouth in shock. They both looked at me and told me not to tell anyone.

I said, "I won't."

He said, "I'll kiss you if you promise not to tell anyone."

I answered okay somewhat hesitantly.

So he walked up put his hands on my shoulders leaned in with his lips pursed and kissed me. My first kiss. Like most first kisses for kids it only lasted a few seconds but that was all I needed.

I looked at my friend and then I walked out down the hall to my after school classroom. There I sat in the desk in front of my friend and turned around.

"I had my first kiss," I whispered to my best friend Serena, "it was Robert."

But even as I shared the so-called good news a part of me wasn't excited. It was my first kiss and though I knew little, or nothing, about love and relationships at six, I knew it wasn't what I wanted. I felt like my first kiss moment was stolen from me.

It was in a coat closet, in the shadows, in the dark. It was a consolation prize for my silence. And was so telling of my future. Many moments of life have not been in coat closets but definitely in the dark, hidden, where I assumed I belonged. Where no one can see me. Where only I keep the secrets. Much like my first kiss, so many secrets and stories have hidden in the shadows. Some moments I feel were stolen, some I did the hiding and sneaking and some just happened, whether I wanted them to or not. It was just reality.

My first kiss was supposed to be a secret. *Charell, you're not supposed to tell anyone. You're an afterthought tossed to the side like an old rag. Anything with you is not to be shown in the light, not to be shared with the world.* From my first kiss I learned that and from my first kiss I lived that life.

My first kiss was not amazing. There was no fairytale romance, and in my life there hasn't been a fairytale romance. But there have been ups and downs, some goods and bads, some fine men some not so fine men, and some funny stories with my family and friends along the way that make up for such an awful first kiss.

***

Relationships, more specifically boys, always had my attention growing up. Only in college did I realize they are not a necessity. I don't need a man, however as a girl all I wanted was a boyfriend. A boyfriend who would validate me, make me worthy and prove to the world I was beautiful and desirable. I had an endless number of middle and high school crushes, black, white and brown it didn't matter. He only had to be cute, the only requirement for a young girl, I wasn't checking for his ambition, salary or retirement plans.

Of all my childhood crushes, I only acted on two of them, both in middle school where some of my worst coming of age moments happened. And I mean everything from period mishaps and cramps to fighting and the stuff in between.

I had a year-long crush on Miles during sixth grade. I was obsessed. He was the cutest thing I had ever seen in all of my 11 years of life. He was caramel like me with hazel eyes. I didn't even know him, but I thought he was cute and there my crush ensued. I had not talked to him all year yet all my classmates knew about my crush. At the end of every school year, the school held a field day on the football field where we could pass around our yearbooks and take pictures before we departed for the summer break. I was standing with my friends and had got the guts to ask Miles to sign my yearbook. I timidly walked up to him and asked, "Miles would you sign my yearbook?" He looked at me and rolled his eyes. His friend, Daniel, a classmate of mine, pushed his shoulder and told him to just do it. He resigned and signed his name with the purple pen I gave him. I thought I wanted his signature, but it was meaningless since it was forced. It was meaningless and useless just like my crush. At that moment my crush was crushed and I no longer had any school-girl feelings towards him.

Although I wasn't crushing on Miles anymore I needed someone else to occupy my attention, right? So seventh grade focused on Richard, a white boy who would probably be classified as punk. He was into skateboarding and shopped at Hot Topic. I had a few classes with him; he was nice and I was mesmerized by his blue eyes. I got up the gumption to write a note, yes a note, these were the days before cell phones. Only a select few kids had cell phones, and those that did were prepaid. Prepaid meant limited messages and minutes for your phone, basically all communication was up to your parents' pocketbooks discretion. My friends and I made folded, football shaped notes to pass around and once even had an entire notebook in rotation purely for our conversations. Our notebook was *GroupMe before GroupMe*. I wrote the note for Richard and one of my friends passed it to him during lunch. I could see him from across the lunchroom open my note, read it, laugh, share it with his friends, and laugh more. I was humiliated and hurt and tears immediately began. I sat with my homemade lunch, packed with love from my mom, and cried over it. I had to get myself together before lunch was over. He came to me after lunch with a quick and firm "no" and that was the end of it.

Middle school crushes taught me one thing: to keep my mouth shut.

When I entered high school, I was there as just another part of life's progression. Then there was a boy who I thought the sun and moon revolved around. He was liked by a lot of my friends too, but I kept quiet and played the supportive friend role. He and I were great friends during high school and became confidants especially regarding our issues with our parents. We both related to being the oldest of our siblings and the pressure that came with it. I spent four years being his friend waiting for him to notice me.

Freshman year was spent learning each other. Bonding over teenage angst and homework problems.

Sophomore year was spent learning I wasn't the only one who liked him.

Junior year was spent watching him try to date my best friend and take her to prom.

Senior year waiting on him to ask me to prom. Instead he asked to join my group of friends as we planned where we would dine before and after the dance.

I spent too much time waiting and wanting someone who didn't want me.

All of my childhood crushes were unrequited. Nobody could

convince me it wasn't because I was fat and ugly. *"Nobody wants me and who could blame them,"* I would think to myself.

College was a different beast. It wasn't insults or crazy crushes, but lack of interest. I was the go-to-girl men talked to for my friends. I was the DUFF- the designated ugly fat friend. My two best friends were gorgeous, each with their own enviable traits. From the large group of a dozen to my triangle of besties- Hilary, Monica and me-I always felt ugly. So much so I would over analyze everything. Thinking my friends would be, and should be, embarrassed of me. I mean, I am embarrassed of myself so why wouldn't they be? And it seems I'll forever be cute. With large round cheeks, (thanks Mom) that make my face warm and welcome with a slight childish tone, I get *"oh you're so cute"* when I get compliments.

Instead of compliments I would field endless queries.

My friends all have whip appeal. Whip appeal is when a man walks past you and turns back around to get another glimpse. The thing that makes a man break his neck trying to watch you walk away.

That's all I ever wanted: whip appeal.

"Hey yo light-skin," men would yell to get my attention.

"Is your friend single?"

"Why she acting like that?"

"If you don't shut up yo mouth," is what I was thinking. *"Talk to her not me, that's who you want, and chumming it up with me doesn't help."*

So often my weight has not only been a crutch its been the what-if. As in, what if it's because I'm fat that nobody likes me? Is that why I don't have whip appeal?

But here's the other side. When I moved to New York and became a target of street harassment, it was bittersweet. I was finally getting the recognition I had always craved, however, I quickly learned that it is not the kind of adoration I wanted. Men yelling and hassling you as you walk to work or the grocery store is far from ideal. It's annoying at best and scary at worst. You may able to laugh it off, but then some men turn and the mouth that once held sweet sentiments now hurls insults faster than ears can comprehend.

I kept wanting and waiting. From elementary, to middle school, to high school and college. Wanting and waiting for some guy to notice me. It took a long time, but I finally figured it out. I was wasting time, wanting, waiting, and wondering if someone would find me worthwhile. I realized all along I needed to find myself valuable.

***

I had been in New York for about a month and was getting my bearings. My friend Lauryn was keeping me in the loop of events and one was a day party in Brooklyn. This was before I even knew what a day party was, I was down for anything, open to trying new things and eager to get out and explore the city.

I went alone hoping she would show. I was still very much closed in and did not want to be a burden to my one friend in the city.

While there I found a corner I could cling to. In the corner were a group of young friends having fun, playing games, and talking. They were nice enough to include me in the conversation, probably sensing I was alone and looking to have a good time.

One of the people was a guy. He was about my height and was handsome. He was kind, asking me about my recent move and what I was doing. Before he left, he offered to take my number to tell me about more events and happenings in the city.

I hesitantly looked at him and he responded I didn't have to give him my number.

I didn't.

I was dumb.

Not every guy who asks for your number wants a relationship, I don't believe in that mindset. But I hate that I felt so little of myself that I wasn't worthy of this man's time. It wasn't nerves, but fear of not being enough. I could have missed out on a good friend or just someone to text me events in NYC, a major key in a city that always has something going on. Instead, I opted out.

I attended an event at the same place in Brooklyn a week later with Lauryn. I was finally seeing I wasn't a burden to friends, that I should open my mouth, communicate more. I told her about the story and lo-and-behold he was there. I pointed him out; she looked at me like I was crazy, and I proceed to my usual modus operandi: avoiding anyone I know and pretending they are not there to dodge conversation. I had made one stride with my friend but I still had more growing to do.

***

When *For Colored Girls* came out I was in college and went to see it with the black student organization on campus. As I try to do, I read the book before the film to know how it would play out and to see how it would be translated on screen. I don't like my first impression of an actual story to be the one I see in theatres or on television. My momma had also read the book as a young girl and ran to the theatre to see it. She called me the opening weekend to discuss the film.

"Did you see *For Colored Girls*?" she asked.

"Yep it was cool," I replied.

"I loved the book. What was your favorite poem?" she asked as we discussed the book versus the movie.

"Um, the one about taking stuff," I answered.

"Oh my god, baby, yes," she said her light voice sounding tinged with sadness. "Yes, I love that one. I never want you to give your stuff away. Give all yourself to someone to be used."

"Mom," I said somewhat exasperated.

"I've done it before. And I don't want you to go through that." She was crying now. I don't like crying and the only thing for me worse than hearing others cry is being the one doing the crying. I couldn't help but think she was talking about my father.

She was right. I have listened to several versions of that poem and each time it resonates with me. I have never given my stuff away to a man and I don't intend to. I had a several year-long crush on a guy in high school and that was too much of me going to a man who didn't even know it. I'm not giving my stuff to a man who won't recognize it. The poem, as all the book *For Colored Girls* does, speaks to a black woman's experience. Resonates on more than a surface level. The entire piece stuck with me and I recall lines regularly from the piece:

> *Somebody almost walked off with all of my stuff*
> *And didn't care enough to send a note home saying I was late for my solo conversation*
> *Or two sizes too small for my own tacky skirts*
>
> *And I was standing there looking at myself the whole time*
> *It wast spirit that ran off with my stuff*
> *It was a man who's ego won't drown like road ants shadow*
> *It was a man faster than my innocence*
> *It was a lover I made too much room for almost ran off with all of my stuff*
> *And the one running with it, don't know he got it*
> *I'm shouting this is mine and he don't, and he don't even know he got it*
> *My stuff is the anonymous ripped off treasure of the year*
> *Did you know somebody almost got away with me!*
> *Me! in a plastic bag under his arm, Me!*

My dad was my mom's first true love. I don't know if she's ever been in love like that since. I hope that she, and my dad, find someone they can love and be with for the rest of their lives.

I want my mom to be happy and keep her stuff. As I looked at their relationship growing up, it solidified what I would and wouldn't do, long before I knew what stuff was or that I had something men would want.

No one is walking off with my stuff.

I was seeking validation from others. If I didn't get their approval then I didn't matter.

Your happiness will never be found in the hands of a man, or anyone else, it is found inside- in the deep crevices of your mind and heart, under sofa cushions next to loose change and bread crumbs, the forgotten places you haven't tended to, the ones that you need to overturn and examine. Your happiness is hidden under the weeds in the garden you let overtake your flowers and rob its beauty. Somedays I wear this knowledge like a badge of honor other days I search for it like a pair of lost keys, unable to remember where I last left them, but knowing I cannot do anything without them. Those days are the toughest, but they pass.

FAMILY PORTRAIT

My parents live in two different worlds
and I'm still trying to figure out how to reside in both

DADDY'S GIRL(S)

Daddy's Little Girl No More:

"You have a sister" he said to me
How does an 11-year-old preteen process such news?
"You have a sister" he told me first, then my brothers
Why me?
Because I was –am?—daddy's little girl
"You have a sister" the oldest and leader of his mixed pack
of six, I guess now, seven, kids
The smart, reasonable, mature one—even at that age
"You have a sister" I didn't bat an eyelash
He spoke so calmly that I just listened
"How do you feel? What are you thinking?" he asked.
I'm still not sure
I think I was just shocked at the moment
I remember saying it's okay, smiling, told him "I guess I
always said I wanted a sister"
But it was too late.
I look back now and feel anger, confusion, love?
"You have a sister" four words rocked my world
No longer daddy's little girl

We had our silly banter
He'd say "You're my favorite daughter in the whole world"
I'd reply "But daddy I'm your only daughter"
The banter has changed and I don't think I like it, but it's
how it is
He says "You're the bestest, my favorite Charell in the
world"
I say nothing
I don't know what to say
Cause I know it's different
I'm not your only daughter so that statement would be
invalid and wrong and hurtful
To her, yes
I've grown a bit
Maybe a lot
My perspective has changed
It's not her fault
But thoughts of my past still bring a twinge of pain
She took my role
It hurt so much to see someone ask my dad as she clung to
his leg "Oh, is she the only girl?"
I stood next to him "No. That was me."
I couldn't help it, emotion came over me
She's here
She's my sister
I can't change that
But I can change me
Be the sister I always wanted for me
Talk to her, laugh, share
Hopefully we'll grow close
As much pain as I felt of my title being lost
Of feeling I was being replaced
I know her life isn't great
Different last name from her siblings

The youngest
Dad lives in a different city now
No siblings to grow up with, laugh with, bicker with, play
with
I know she's missing out
Is it possible we both got the short end of the stick?
Thanks to our dad who couldn't control his---
Mmm, nope, let's not, he's not perfect, he's human and he's
another poem
I see her life and feel bad for my initial offense
I had him as a child
She doesn't
I had our brothers
She doesn't
We'd play all the time
Piggy back rides were my favorite
Our song was "Ain't no sunshine when she's gone"
What's theirs?
They probably don't have one
Is she lonely?
Her mom's only child
Wow this isn't a competition of who has it worse or better
Both are out of some sort of luck, or something
I hope we can grow together
Form a bond
Where my pain and resentment are erased
And she develops none
And together we become more than sisters
We become friends
And share the title
We'll be Daddy's Little Girls

I wrote that years ago, I'm really not sure when. I've never thought my poetry has ever been great, but that doesn't keep me from writing it. Writing seems to have always been a part of my life in some form or fashion. I have poems, random journals and started several stories. I'm not a writer that constantly puts pen to paper, but it helps to write sometimes, as it is the best way to articulate how I feel at a specific moment. In that moment I still wrestled with my familial changes.

***

Growing up the only girl was my claim to fame. In a house full of boys I was unique. My daddy would say, "You're my favorite daughter," to which I would sigh roll my eyes and respond, "I'm your only daughter daddy." I acted exasperated, but I really loved it, it was nice to be recognized, set apart and I always felt special. Though I am older than my brothers, I always felt protected, like they had my back, we were a team, a unit, a family, as odd as we were. I proudly boasted in classes, "I am the oldest of six kids and the only girl." It's what I used to make me special.

When I was 11 years old that all changed.

Daddy called me into his room to talk.

He had just gotten married a month ago to Dionne, who I really liked, but after their honeymoon, I didn't see her again. They were taking time apart, but I didn't know why.

"I have something to tell you," he said. "You have a sister. She's one year old and her name is Jamison. I wanted to make sure of a few things first and this was not expected but you have a sister. Dionne and I are getting divorced and that's how it will go. You and your brothers will get to meet your new sister soon."

A lot of adults in my life spoke to me as an adult, even while a child. They didn't have to mince words as they knew I had a good grasp on situations, after all *"that baby ain't missed nothing"* right?

He said he wanted to tell me first, talk about it. After all, I'm the oldest and probably because I was the only girl of the gang.

To see how I reacted, if I had questions or thoughts. I was probably too in shock to have questions. And just hearing the news how would I know what changes would take place?

I handled it well. Often my responses are one of two: I have an immediate reaction and act on impulse or I haven't fully processed it and will respond in kind, not knowing until later what my actual feelings were. At this instance, I was the latter. I told him, "Daddy, I don't really know what to say. I mean I guess I always wanted a sister."

I used to always wish and pray for a sister, then I got one, just a little too late. I had already settled into being sisterless and the thought of someone else in my family was incomprehensible.

I remember when we first met.

Jamison's mom, Leslie, brought her over to the house. She was a chunky baby with soft curly brown hair, yellow skin and she was also cursed with Daddy's eyebrows. I don't know how genetics work, but I swear girls always get the short end of the stick. My brothers are walking around with long eyelashes, curly hair, and fast metabolisms, however, me not so much. Daddy's eyebrows are peculiar, and it seemed as if Jamison would be the other kid to inherit them right along with me. Our eyebrows start off in a box shape and then abruptly cut off into a blunt line. They're not ridiculously full but hairy enough to be annoying, and I constantly have to let every person who waxes or threads my eyebrows know hair doesn't grow in certain areas, nothing happened but genetics.

I sat with Jamison and one of my little brothers. Her mom was hesitant to leave her so she could talk to my dad. I quickly told her I was no stranger to babies or changing diapers she'll be fine. I sat with my new sister and we pretty much looked at each other. I couldn't really do much, she was a baby after all. My dad took a picture of the both of us together on his flip phone.

Since our first meeting I've tried to build a relationship with her but I have been unsuccessful. Part of me wonders if it's me or her, or if we will ever be more than blood relatives. I thought sisters were supposed to be your best friends.

During my college breaks we would go on movie dates together, Leslie always willing to coordinate schedules with me. In college, I wrote her pen-pal letters, called, and I always sent her birthday cards and Christmas gifts. It wasn't much, but it's what I could do. When I graduated college and lived at home for a few months, I attended her sporting games. But talking to my sister is like pulling teeth. I wasn't sure if it was me or her being socially awkward, but we have yet to click.

When one of our brothers graduated college, my dad got Jamison and me a hotel room together. I said to myself, *"I will give this one more try, hopefully, we'll get to connect while we're in the hotel."* Instead, she was in my dad's room the entire night talking with him. I felt torn. I understand her need and want to be with daddy. I grew up with him, she isn't. She doesn't have the same relationship and hasn't spent the same time with him I did as a kid. I can't fault her for that. But it still hurts to feel you may never have a relationship with someone you're related to, especially your only sister in the world.

As the oldest, I often feel a strong pull to lead my siblings in love. To have a relationship with each of them. Sometimes I fail and sometimes I succeed, but I never stop trying.

My sister is now a teenager and I'm not sure when, if ever, we will have a conversation and form those sisterly bonds I've heard so much about. I had to learn not to compare myself to her. That we are two different individuals with our own lives to live. I am unique, and though I love my family more than anything, there's more than just that. I don't need to rely on them to make me stand out. I lost nothing when I found out I had a sister. Instead, I gained another family member. Another person to love.

LETTER TO MY SISTER

Sister,

Even though I wasn't there throughout your childhood, I want you to know that I tried. Did my best to show up and remember the important days. Know that I love you and think of you often. We may not ever be friends, but we will always be family.

Love,

Your Sissy
(You may not remember when you called me that with a face full of love, but I do.)

THE F-WORD

My grandma Melanie cooking dinner for her family. Laboring in love- full bellies her method of spreading warmth.

My grandma Linda who left her husband and father of her four sons and found love elsewhere with a younger man.

My grandma Melanie who left her husband and father of her three daughters and found love elsewhere with a younger man.

My mom with four kids from a man she would never marry. Four kids, with faces of the man she would never marry, looking to her daily for love and attention. She gave it unconditionally.

My aunt Irene who decided she didn't want to be a mother but would be a kick-ass aunt.

My aunt Celestine who was and still is a fighter. Dukes up for anyone who disrespects or threatens her family.

My grandma Linda returning to school in her forties and getting her college degree.

My mother returning to school in her forties and getting her college degree.

Daily acts and decisions of living your best self. I learned from them and grew from there.

That's what feminism is, at least for me.

***

When I turned 18 my grandmother wanted to buy me sapphire jewelry. Sapphire's were one of the first nice pieces of jewelry she ever got to own for herself, and she was grown with three kids when she did. The story goes one night my grandpa came home drunk and made her beyond mad. She took his wallet and the money in it and bought herself a sapphire ring. This was the first, but not the last time, she would help herself to her husband's wallet to buy herself a nice piece of jewelry.

Bobby said to her, "You are a Sapphire lady, huh?" Using the word sapphire instead of bitch when he sobered up and noticed the missing money and her new jewelry.

She responded, "I sure am."

She was strong, unapologetic and flashy. And she wanted to make sure I knew I was too. She said I want you to be a sapphire lady, meaning *we ain't taking nothing from nobody and you can do whatever you want.* We went to the Zales counter at a local mall and found a heart necklace made of sapphires in the clearance section. It was the first piece of jewelry I could remember receiving since childhood. It was new and all mine. I held the small heart in my hands looking at the pink and white stones settled in their silver casing. I felt important, special and loved. I wanted to be a sapphire lady too. Grandma did what she wanted and I would too.

Before I knew what feminism was, or the caricature of Sapphire, I knew my family, and especially my grandmother Melanie. I knew she was a woman who worked hard, enjoyed life, loved others and gave of herself unselfishly. I learned that a woman can be independent and strong-willed and married and be a good mother and work and make her own money and manage family finances. I saw a multi-dimensional woman, and I saw that I too could be as layered and complex and still be whole.

I come from strong women, like many do. I also come from strong men, like many do. I come from a family where strong women and strong men were in relationships, good, bad or indifferent, and I learned. The relationships of my parents and grandparents was not traditional. There was respect, there were boundaries, and each person was allowed to have their own strengths and weaknesses that, in turn, their partner could fill. Gender-roles are bullshit. I learned from my family that my rhetoric was not void of value. I had a voice, and I had to use it to amplify the issues that matter to me as best as possible.

Before I knew what misogyny was, I knew things just didn't add up. As a child, you notice small inequalities and the older you get the bigger the inequities are.

My brand of feminism isn't store bought.

It's not pretty.

It's as complicated and complex as I am.

I'm a woman that cheers for other women.

I recognize my privilege that being a college educated, cisgender, heterosexual woman gives me.

I recognize intersectionality, for me, it is that of being black and woman.

I see my strengths and weaknesses.

I'm new to this feminism thing, at least the label. I couldn't find myself in feminism. I had read no books, and I still have a lot more learning to do. But I know how I felt and what I wanted to see change. You don't have to be a scholar, or even a woman, to understand the issues with the status quo (this can be said for racial issues as well, see there is intersectionality everywhere).

I couldn't get through Lean In by Sheryl Sandberg. It didn't appeal to me, I couldn't see myself in the pages. I couldn't get behind Taylor Swift. To me, she was fraudulent and represented everything I grew to understand feminism as: exclusionary, beneficial to only white women, and silencing of others. On the other hand, I could breeze through Year of Yes by Shonda Rhimes. I could understand Janet Mock and Roxanne Gay. And as I delve more into this world, I will encounter more people I relate to and others I don't. I see that there are many varying opinions. Beyoncé's brand of feminism doesn't match everyone's and has been criticized. Her feminism is fit into a leotard showcasing her body for all the world to see. Its 24-inch blonde weave, while being happily married, having a child at her personal time of choosing, while strategically plotting, planning and working hard at her profession. Through all this, she has never lost her Texas drawl and regularly rocks cornrows and grills. She's the boss, and not everyone is fond of the CEO. Beyoncé's feminism I could relate to. It seemed tangible and was easy to understand. She was like me; she seemed to be for women and black women particularly. She wasn't perfect, and not above reproach, but she was also the complex layered woman I could see myself in. I was grasping this whole feminism thing and finding my space in it.

***

But it is not about constant talk of theories and role models, its life that really matters. Our days, and how you must navigate and handle it being a woman. Facing those inequalities or daily nuances of a male dominated world.

Some days are good and others hurt. The day I found out that my brother probably doesn't respect me as a woman was one of those days that hurt. Hit me deep and I haven't been the same since. When someone you would take a bullet for seems to have zero respect for you it makes you re-evaluate everything.

My brother, I'm not telling which one, has very archaic ideas of what a woman's role is. It's not his archaic thoughts that are the most astounding, it's that we were raised in the same house with the same values and lessons from our parents and grandparents and some kind of twisted way he drew this conclusion. The conclusion that a woman must cook and clean and be docile though every woman who raised us worked one, if not multiple jobs, and was a major contributor to the household. Despite the fact that my grandpa knew there were lines he was not to cross with his wife. Despite the fact that Bobby did the laundry in addition to yard work. The fact that grandma could roll weed, cuss like a sailor and hold her own with men on the spades table or the street. She never turned down help, but she knew she didn't need to rely on anyone to be okay. Despite this, his views are contrary to our upbringing. That's what is astounding.

Recently I saw one of his status updates come across my social media timeline. Another slew of words meant to discredit women's petitions for equality. His rhetoric is not just controversial, it's dangerous. Seems he feels like a woman should know her place. But I feel a woman's place is anywhere she wants it to be.

I must clarify that I have no doubt he loves me. I've learned that love and like are two very different things. Just as love and respect are two different things. And each can reside individually, they are all mutually exclusive.

He loves his sister who he grew up with. The sister who is making a way for herself, and no matter how much family arguing there is will present a united front when facing a threat or enemy to the family. He would take a bullet for me too, I have no doubt.

However, he doesn't like my thoughts and opinions that spill freely and unapologetically from my mouth. My opinions hold no weight for him. They are of no significance. What could I tell him that has any value?

When I came to that realization, it not only stung, it was

heart crushing. And he is so stubborn in his ideas he cannot see its absurdness, my other siblings can see the crazy rhetoric he spits for what it is- utter ludicrousness.

My brother's stance doesn't make me cower, no, on the contrary, it forces me to really examine my beliefs and stances. I have to explain why my points are valid and entertain audiences with opposing views.

Why does my owning and claiming my inner power offend you? Disgust you? Why do you sigh in resignation? I do not understand.

Little does my brother know he lit a fire under me, and for that, I strangely love him a bit more.

***

When I started Strong and Elite (S+E) the hardest part was coming up with a name. I had a running list of names from Black Elite (taken and too exclusionary for me at the time), Ebony Elite, Urban Elite, etc. and I gave up. I landed on Strong, incorporating my last name and adding Elite to it. I figured I wouldn't have to worry about copyright issues, since it's my name after all, and why not attribute two powerful words to women. I don't know how long I will run S+E, if it's a company for life or for a season, but I know it has allowed me to grow and do things I never thought I would. It has allowed me to examine my viewpoint and effectively articulate it. It has given my voice a home outside of myself where others are welcome to visit.

Being a woman is a balancing act. And though my company is called Strong and Elite I work to make sure that women don't feel pressure to be strong all the time, but to know they have inner strength. That they can achieve they can imagine. The strong black woman archetype is real but can also be our downfall. *For Colored Girls who have Considered Suicide* showed us there's no prerequisite to feel grief, pain, or despair. I think at some point we've all wanted to disappear. Be swallowed by the earth. Fade to black surrounded by nothing but darkness.

To escape. Or breathe. Or just be done. Cause we are tired. Beyoncé (can you tell I'm a fan) leaped from a building in the beginning of her Lemonade visual album. The image is jarring, but it's also real. I've been there mentally and emotionally before, wanting to call it quits. There is a pressure to be a strong black woman while simultaneously fighting the negative connotations of an angry black woman. Strength doesn't mean you don't have weaknesses. Weaknesses and failures and upsets are fine. It's human. Vulnerability is powerful, it is a capacity some are not fortunate to allow themselves to possess or experience, find the power in being open. To receive love, give love and to prosper I've found that I need to be vulnerable. The strength is having the confidence to open yourself up to others to learn, grow, love and even be heartbroken or disappointed. It takes power. Everything from love, to self-confidence, to vulnerability is really a culmination to being the best you.

***

I didn't want to be called a feminist. It was a dirty word. Being called a feminist meant I might be seen as a bald, braless, hairy man-hater. Somewhere society taught me that to be named a feminist was an insult, something to make you hang your head in shame.

Now, call me what you want and I'll wear it as a badge. Right now, I prefer not to title myself as I see that I value equity, equality and the variety of voices that women have to input to the conversation. Labels can limit and restrict the commentary you allow yourself to indulge in. I don't mind being labeled by others because it means that you understand or slightly grasp what I am trying to accomplish -whether you are agreeing or hurling an insult at me is not my concern.

Feminism. Womanism. Humanism. Whatever word you want to tack an –ism behind doesn't matter.

It's the values and lessons I learned that brought me to this conclusion.

That owning my wholeness is not only okay, it's necessary. That you can leave a man whenever the fuck you want with no apologies, and you can stay too with no apologies. That finding your power doesn't take away from anyone else's, especially a man's.

Being a woman is one of the most difficult and most magnificent things in the world. So if it makes you feel better you can call me the F-word.

MY BLACK RENAISSANCE

If you spend your life trying to figure out who everyone
else is
Be who everyone else is
You'll never have time to discover who it is
You are

Growing up obsessed with fashion led to my obsession with magazines. Teen magazines specifically, like *Cosmo Girl*, *Seventeen*, *Teen Vogue*, *Teen People*, *YM*, the list goes on and on. However, each of these magazines had an issue with representation. When there was a black girl she was often racially ambiguous or had light-skin with green eyes and silky baby hairs to match. I could do none of the suggested makeup and style tips with my coarse hair and large frame. Realizing I subscribed to magazines with a lack of overall diversity is jarring, there was little representation and it undoubtedly effected my psyche.

Whether verbally or through imagery, some types of beauty are never questioned, they are merely accepted as fact. I find it is often easier to accept yourself as beautiful when the world and everything and everyone around you affirms it.

I, on the other hand, had neither, the world or my inner circle, as a young child to constantly affirm my beauty. Maybe we had bigger issues to worry about, which we did. Maybe we valued education over vanity, which we do. Maybe my family didn't think it necessary. Regardless of the reasons, growing up I never felt pretty.

Like most girls, my standard of beauty derived from the woman I saw the most, the one who undoubtedly has the largest impact on a girl's life, my mother. My mother was the epitome of beauty to me. She had hazel eyes, light skin, petite features and long, thick hair. It seemed I had gained none of her traits in the genetic lottery. Even my grandmother faced these challenges. I remember her telling me how she also wanted to be beautiful like her mother. My grandmother and I look similar, with caramel skin, brown eyes, and coarse hair, only she had a distinguishable gap in her mouth while my pearly whites are uninterrupted. My great-grandmother was light, very light, a woman that could undoubtedly pass the paper bag test, and she had light eyes. Her features were and still are family traits that someone in every generation has inherited in some form or fashion. As a kid, the only people you see naked are your parents for bath time and changing clothes. My grandmother saw that her mother's nipples were very light, while her areolas were dark brown. She didn't know why they were different, just that they were. To look like her mother, my grandmother used bleaching cream to lighten her nipples. You can probably imagine how successful this was, it wasn't. She burned her skin with the cream. Lesson learned. My grandmother faced internal challenges in her youth but she grew to be secure and confident in herself. Me, I was still growing.

A lack of affirmation led to me seeking it from others. From friends, boys, anyone who would notice me. And when I couldn't have my beauty, I always had my brain, hiding behind the confidence that someone may be prettier but they couldn't be smarter than me. It seemed a woman could be only two things in my world: beautiful or smart. If I couldn't be beautiful I would make damn sure I was smart. Right? Wrong. My awkward years were just that, awkward. From my hair to my clothes to my body and everything in between I really had to grow into myself and now I finally feel a semblance of control and authority over my body.

I had a low amount of self-worth. I still tend to rely on the power of my mind because you can't take that away from me. Beauty is relative. But my mind can easily be weighed against others to determine its significance whereas my beauty not so much. I was not confident in my beauty. I didn't believe someone could find me beautiful for a long time.

***

Throughout my life, like most people, I received compliments based on my outward appearance. However, I also received more than a fair amount of backhanded compliments. They usually went along the lines of, *"You are a beautiful girl but if you just lost some weight..."* The sting of that kind of compliment was the worst. Words last like a tender spot on your scalp, its always there and the slightest pressure causes pain. The first time I actually felt beautiful with no doubts was my Cotillion.

Cotillion is an annual scholarship program run by Delta Sigma Theta Sorority, Inc. a historically black sorority based on sisterhood, scholarship, and service. My godmother, beautician and a few of my mother's friends were in the local chapter and sponsored me to take part. I initially had no interest in Cotillion. I was focused on making it to debate nationals and getting a good GPA to finish high school with some pride. My mother really wanted me to participate and she would make it happen. The program was very simply structured, high school seniors participated throughout the school year in a variety of activities to earn scholarship money. You paid a fee to participate, but everyone was guaranteed to get that money back as a scholarship. We were expected to do community service, write an essay on a given subject, attend a college tour and take part in a talent show. The culmination of all of these activities would be celebrated in May with a Cotillion, a formal event, similar to a coming out ceremony, where our accomplishments from high school were shared. The most unique part is that the ceremony was formal. The male participants would wear tuxedos and the ladies would have white gowns and gloves. Our parents would walk out with us and we performed a waltz.

The day of Cotillion, as most teenagers are, we were ready to get it over with. We had spent the previous day practicing our waltz and finale dance and were ready to relax. The girls and guys were all sent to various rooms in the hotel venue to change and get dressed. A local gown boutique custom fit our dresses and they were on site to assist in any way needed.

I did my makeup, which was a simple routine now that I look back, but then I knew my makeup skills were impeccable. After learning the ropes from my former debate partner and friends Symone and Freddie, I knew how to get it right. It was eyeshadow, mascara, foundation and blush with a little lip gloss. Fancy right? We all changed into our white ball gowns complete with white tights, shoes, gloves, pearl earrings and a pearl necklace. To finish the look, we also received a tiara. We were young black queens. Every girl looked beautiful in her dress and every guy looked handsome in his tuxedo.

We proceeded to the ballroom for photos and to begin the ceremony, which started after a formal dinner for the attendees. Each student was accompanied by their parents as they were introduced and their accolades were shared. The program then announced winners for all the tasks we had completed throughout the process. I won for best essay and was awarded additional scholarship money. After the award announcements participants performed a waltz with their parents, the ladies with their fathers and young men with their mothers, and then the finale dance. After the ceremony, there was a chaperoned after party in the hotel. There was a DJ and all the participants could dance and celebrate making it through the process and moving on to other things, we still had prom and graduation to look forward to.

I had so much support that night; I felt loved, which I'm sure added to my feeling beautiful. My family was there and several church family members were in attendance, with two other ladies from my church taking part in Cotillion, there was no shortage of love and support. One of my mom's friends from high school was the emcee and he mentioned how old he was getting introducing his classmate's children. My hometown is big and small at the same time and Cotillion was a perfect example of this. I was surrounded by people I had known my entire life and could still meet people I had never run into and find out we had common friends and interests. I even discovered I was a distant relative of one participant, her grandmother and mine were cousins and grew up together- we had the same great-great-great grandmother. Of course, I didn't make this connection, my mother the social butterfly did.

That night after the event when I came home my grandma and aunt were still up talking about the event. I remember them agreeing on how profound Cotillion was, glad I could participate. That black children, many descendants of slaves, were in a ballroom waltzing. *Who would have ever conceived of something so beautiful happening?* They kept gushing that my photos from that night, and the one in the official Cotillion program, would be ones I would show my children one day. Pictures where I could say, *"look how beautiful I was when I was young."* I didn't agree about my program photograph but I definitely felt beautiful that night.

As I look back my grandmother and aunt were absolutely right. There is something undeniably beautiful and powerful in the image of black youth waltzing with their parents. The descendants of people who used to watch others dance and clean up after them, unable to look up, we had our heads up and arms out proud. Even more, the entire mission of the program is phenomenal. To open youth up to meeting students from other schools, visiting colleges and the overall experience. I could not take part fully due to my school commitments, but what I could do was great, and I do not have one bad memory of my entire Cotillion experience.

I am so glad to have shared that moment with my mom, dad and both of my grandmothers. The four people responsible for my existence and two of which I know have prayed for me more than I have ever prayed for myself. That night was one of the best in my 17 years. I was finally growing into myself, becoming bold and fearless, getting a taste of what life could be with a change of perspective.

Cotillion was the first time I felt beautiful.

The first time I believed it?

I'm not sure I have yet.

I was reminded of the growing I still have to do when I arrived home from New York for the holidays. Talking with my aunt and one my oldest friends, Symone, about life and catching up. We talked about everything from work, society, family to relationships. It is this last topic that gets my friend and me every time. We are both young, and though she has dated more than me, are both tired of the hopelessness dating as a millennial seems to offer. We talked in depth about dating, or my lack thereof. They both said I should open myself up and go out more to meet people. All fine, things that are a little tough to accept but not life altering. Then my aunt said, "I don't think you believe you are beautiful, deep down I think you still struggle." Inside I paused because she is right and it's a sad revelation I still haven't grown enough. It is this conversation that gave me a stark reminder that though I have had moments where I *felt* beautiful I didn't *believe* I was. There is a difference.

***

In terms of love and relationships, loving yourself is probably the hardest thing to do and the most important for living a satisfied life. In complete transparency, I am still on my journey of loving myself wholly, and I've come far but I realize there is still a long way to go. There are good days, where I cross an invisible threshold in my mind of personal acceptance, and bad days. Every one of us is at a different point in our lives that may cause us to question who we are and why we are valuable.

There are many aspects to self-acceptance and one of them is knowing comparison destroys contentment. How often have you looked at your Instagram news feed and had negative thoughts? *Why is she so gorgeous? Why can't I do that? Why doesn't my hair look like that? Why can't I afford to live that way?* We find ourselves instantly comparing our lives to someone else's social media profile. As I once heard, don't compare your behind the scenes to someone else's highlight reel. Social media is surface, and we only share the good. Seeing someone's smiling photo does not reveal to you the personal struggles they are encountering or the everyday challenges they face. By comparing yourself to others you leave yourself open to constant disappointment- you'll never measure up because you'll always desire to be like someone else.

As much as we hear it we must take it to heart: we are all different and it is those differences that make each of us special and necessary to the world. Instead of focusing on the *WHY* focus on the *WHAT*. What makes you unique? What do you like most about yourself? What in your life is going well? I challenge you to begin to focus on the *WHAT*. When you find yourself making comparisons close the app and change your thoughts to center on you. It's okay to be selfish when it comes to loving you.

As for me, I'm starting not to recognize me anymore. This new creature is carrying a place in this world without me. I don't recognize her yet, but I like who I'm becoming.

WRITER'S BLOCK

I'm trying to figure out how to write about my skin.

I'm trying to figure out this skin I'm in.

I still struggle to find the words to explain my blackness. Like my vocabulary isn't vast enough to cover it. And my feelings are so varied from awkwardness and animosity to pride and joy-I don't want my words to be misconstrued.

It is so hard to write about race because it is so hard to live black. I'm not even talking the woman part.

The skin I live in and love others hate, or fear. They can't make sense of it and rather than understand they try to eliminate it. Perceive my skin as a threat. Or maybe, they see its potential, which is even more frightening to them.

We create the cool and someone else profits from it. Tell us it's no good until they say so.

But this fear and confusion in me ain't from my skin, it's from them. I'm working from the outside in to figure me out, this skin out. Cause that's how the world's been set up for me.

There are phases to this. Phases to uncovering your blackness. At least for me it was. We know I've struggled with beauty and its images, and really it's all a massive ball of fuckery, excuse my language.

The images you see are not of you so they breed self-hate at the highest level and self-doubt at the lowest.

I loathed myself. For being fat and nappy we know, but also being black.

Everything in society teaches you to hate yourself. Shows you as inferior. And I internalized those lessons counting them as true regarding me.

But then there is an awakening.

The awakening: it's subconscious, and happens over time.

I'm black. As a child and adolescent, it was just that, an undisputable fact, like saying the sky is blue.

I'm black. As a teenager it becomes some identifying marker, separating you from others. Another physical trait like brown eyes and being tall.

I'm black. As an adult, I have learned it is a condition. It's beautiful and dangerous to be in this body. Empowering in its strength and frightening in its vulnerability.

I'm black. I accept all of me in this skin.

My skin is a marker, it identifies me before I even open my mouth. More so than anything else it is my skin color people notice first. Don't you? When you meet someone you see their skin and gender. Everything else comes after that. My religion, my sexual orientation, my class, my level of education all comes after you know my race and gender. I don't walk into a room and people think look at the middle-class, college educated, cisgender, heterosexual, Christian woman.

It is my skin they see.

The skin I struggle to find words to explains the vastness of.

The skin I'm still trying to live in.

The skin I'm still trying to figure out how to write about.

DON'T LET THE SUN GO DOWN

I live in a world inherently set up for me to fail.
But I defy the odds.

Nigger Don't Let the Sun go Down on Your Ass!

In big bold letters posted up on a sign leading to the main road of a small town or in the town center was what my great-great-grandfather was greeted with when he traveled. My grandma Melanie would tell me stories of how her grandpa would travel, as a small farm owner, and see those exact words posted. A staunch warning- your black behind isn't welcome here and we will kill you. Sundown Towns were real, prevalent across America and though the signs are gone, the mentality is not and there's not anything you can do to protect yourself from that kind of blatant hate.

Melanie was not exempt from situations of hate either. My grandmother never drank out of straws. Throughout my entire life with her we would go to restaurants and she would promptly remove the straw from her beverage before drinking. Why? When she was a kid, a white classmate of hers gave her a straw to use in her drink. The little boy had stuck a dead fly in

127

the straw, and when she drank, she slurped up the fly with her pop. What was not only a disgusting experience, scarred her mentally and left a lasting impression on her- she never drank out of a straw again. So what, it's a bug, what's the big deal? The fly was the symbol of hate used to hurt a child. Racism doesn't have to be blatant murders its big and small every day encounters that shape the way people of color move in the world.

My skin is in constant opposition with the world. From my hair that refuses to lie flat to my brownness that stands out in a crowd. There is no such thing as perfect assimilation.

***

The policing of communities, the black community specifically, varies from daily acts such as hair and clothing to larger scale such as child rearing, public speaking, writing and more. Nothing is safe from critique. From Trayvon Martin's hoodie, to loud music, to simply asking for help nothing you do or say makes you immune to an officer or vigilante's bullet. The idea that you can somehow change internally or externally to prevent hateful acts targeted towards you is a falsehood and a main component of respectability politics. Respectability politics is defined as the policing of the marginalized group by others in the marginalized group. It is the idea that changing your vernacular or dressing a certain way will stop you from being unjustly profiled; it is a common fallacy among the black community. It's what explains why you may hear someone say *"if he hadn't dressed like a thug"* or the public saying *"if she hadn't worn that skirt she wouldn't have been raped."* The knowledge of respectability politics rose with Trayvon and continued on with each chronicled death of an unarmed black man. Respectability politics spans race, gender, and class. The danger is that it places the blame on the victim not the culprit of the insult, injustice or assault. It is often a conditioning from our households. Things we are taught that should be lifesaving, but the wrong lessons are being taught to the wrong audience.

I and many in my generation were raised with the belief we had our rights. We were taught about the sixties Civil Rights Movement and the victories - for all intents and purposes we won. Right? Brown vs. Board of Education, The Voting Rights Act, the Montgomery Bus Boycott, the March on Selma, Freedom Rides, etc. So much pain, so much death, so much sacrifice for us. We were taught that those sacrifices were for the freedoms we now enjoyed- integrated schools, voting rights, shared communal spaces, and more.

However, we should have seen that it was not over. The constant griping of heritage months for people who aren't white, the confederate flag that hangs proudly in several southern states and is for sale in major stores in various forms of paraphernalia. The daily micro-aggressions and subsequent increased criminalization of black bodies.

The death of Trayvon Martin hit us all. It was as if all the indiscretions we experienced–and had written off as minor or one-off incidents- were now valid, that there was a bigger problem that had to be addressed. There was an entire system we seemingly forgot needed to be dismantled. A system that had been built brick by brick to destroy black bodies. A system that from its creation has excluded the freedom of brown people: from the inception of slavery to the unfair labor of sharecroppers to the Jim Crow south to unfair housing acts to the 1994 crime bill and everything in between.

We were never playing a fair game and the death of Trayvon Martin is a marker in the movement. Yes, there were deaths before that, Amadou Diallo, Oscar Grant, Sean Bell but it seems Trayvon's murder, and subsequent unfair villainizing media coverage, struck a chord.

After Trayvon's death, there was a slight reprieve, at least from a mass media perspective. Then came the death of Eric Garner. And Mike Brown. Then the University of Missouri

(Mizzou) protests. It seemed never ending and I could relate to each one in some form or fashion. Not just that I had young brothers like Trayvon, but these were places I knew. St. Louis was where my dad, little brothers and family and friends lived. I went to school in Columbia, heck I even knew a couple of the people protesting at Mizzou. And New York, the place I resided, known for its progressiveness, was now at the center of the Black Lives Matter movement, a center of injustice for the time being. My heart was hurting. If the death of Trayvon was the match, the death of Miles Brown struck and started the flame. Respectability politics be damned, here was a boy from a rough neighborhood of St. Louis, a place I often consider my second home, who was gunned down. He was no one's idea of a sweet little boy yet we all mourned for him, and his loss became the black community's loss. There seemed to be a mass awakening.

Then, there was the video of a young black girl in a bikini being manhandled, as if she could ever take on the officer more than twice her size. She was being unnecessarily violently handled. It was another video of the brutalization of a black body for the world to view, share, and comment on hundreds of thousands of times. After the death of Walter Scott, who was shot in the back at point-blank range, I made a conscious decision to no longer view any videos of police brutality. I would not partake in the watching of a person being dehumanized, humiliated, or taking their last breath on earth. American society, society as a whole, has an unnatural desensitization to violence. We see death, blood and gore so regularly in our entertainment we aren't able to separate fact from fiction. Everything is for consumption- even someone's most vulnerable moments. I could no longer consume the meal of my people's demise.

***

In the past decade, there has been a resurgence of a modern day civil rights movement a la Black Lives Matter. What started as a hashtag has morphed into multiple organizations, protests and a way for everyone to lend their voice on the internet to the movement.

As technology and social media have expanded so has the individual citizen's voice. We are all able to use our small platforms to collectively make a lot of noise. Cell phones also have captured what has been going on for years, the unfair and crooked practices and prejudices that people of color face every day. The body count of black men, black women, queer and trans women continues to rise and with each one we become louder, more restless. We are losing our ability to cope and to code switch as easily as we once could. To wear our masks daily doesn't come as easily. To go into work like everything is okay when we are likely victims of some form of PTSD from seeing so many black lives being taken on film is not a simple task. This shit just ain't easy.

There's so many ways life in America has been set up to destroy and control the black body that books and classes and documentaries have been dedicated to it. No part of the original fabric of America was designed to see blacks excel. Yet despite all that, we endure and break barriers and exceed our own expectations. We still set trends and create art and science and technology that impacts the world. We still find reasons to dance and be filled with joy. As Maya Angelou so beautifully stated, we are the hope and the dream of the slave. The sun can never go down on us, we are the light.

DEAR BLACK GIRL

Dear Black Girl,

I want you to remember.

You are everything! To focus on the good and learn from the bad. Life is about the lessons you learn along the way, not the final destination.

Remember that days differ and they do not determine your value or your final outcome. There are days where the world is your footstool. You know every answer to every question and your light shines through to the world, nearly blinding. And I'm sure there are days where you feel like a stranger in your skin. Your hair won't curl right and it seems like your body is determined to betray you. You can't get anything correct and you want to give up. This too shall pass. I wish I could tell you it will get easier, but I don't believe in false promises. Things may not get easy quickly, but you will become stronger, better adept at handling problems.

Remember there is a line of black women behind you cheering you on. We are your personal pep squad and we only want to see you win. We are your foundation, breaking barriers, cooking meals, solving problems to clear a path for you. We want you to walk the path and go beyond it to continue it for another little black girl.

Remember your beauty, many times unvalued and unaccepted in the world. You are extraterrestrial, your very being defies logic. Your hair defies gravity and your skin contains the sun in even the darkest of places. Your curves and edges, soft and sharp at the same time, are able to provide warmth in a hug and strength to protect itself. Remember you are a masterpiece.

Remember your knowledge. That it goes beyond knowing an answer to a math problem. That it is your instincts that guide you. Your wisdom that lets you learn from others. Your life experiences that shape your mind. Your intelligence cannot be measured by a test, it is innate, it is a lived experience, it is earned and it is yours.

Most importantly remember, you are worth it and your success is inevitable. Whenever you begin to doubt, or your hope waivers, stop, breathe and remember it is possible. It's possible for you.

Love,

A (Former) Black Girl, now a (Young) Black Woman

BLACK WOMAN

She wakes the same as before
Not quite the world's standard of beauty
But beautiful nonetheless
She's open
Her eyes, her heart, her mind
She's loud
Her body, her laugh, her hair, her skin
She protests daily
Besides, what could be more radical than loving yourself?
You Revolutionary Woman

BLACK WOMAN PART DEUX

Black Baby Girl then
Little Black Girl then
Young Black Girl then
Black Woman.
Finding her place in the world is a challenge.
She's navigating in a world that presses on her from all sides.
That shows her no reprieve.
Forces her to be strong then condemns her for her strength.
That is my plight, my cross to bear.
The same one that many other women likely carry.
We try to be soft and hard.
We must be soft and hard.
Often silenced yet our voices are necessary.
The world needs our song.
These hymns can't make themselves.
Men can't make themselves.
We are the secret. The key. The final touch.
Without us the sauce just don't taste right.
Black woman don't need to find her place in the world.
She is the world.

QUARTER CENTURY

26.
Young.
Broke.
Single.
Trying to figure out this thing called life.

As I am writing this, I am having a quarter life crisis. If I'm being all the way honest with you this crisis has been going on and off for the past few years. Endless peaks and valleys. My priorities are paying my rent, keeping my phone on, and having money on my MetroCard. Notice my top three priorities do not include food. That's how real it is right now. Food is definitely in the top ten, make no mistake, but I have to keep my basic bills paid and food ain't a bill.

I call home semi-regularly, needing to hear the voice of someone I know loves me. The voice of someone who knows me. Voices from home cover me, make me warm inside, and remind me I'm not as alone as I feel. My aunt consoles me, says that everyone in their twenties is broke. It sure doesn't feel like it. I just got off Instagram and saw someone return from their trip to Colombia while someone else in GroupMe is copping an error fare to Paris. Me? I'm trying to cop my fare for the subway, $2.75 to be exact, and my bank just emailed me that my balance fell below $25 like I haven't been counting every cent to avoid overdraft. Seems like I'm the only one out here broke. Trying to figure out this thing called life.

Should I go back to school?

Should I change careers?

Should I move across the country again?

What am I doing with my life?

Did I file my taxes correctly? Cause TurboTax keeps sending me emails.

Do I need this last glass of wine? That one was easy, yes I need that glass of wine.

Social media is a facade. It's paradise. It is meant to show the good moments of life. Who wants to share or see someone else's Final Payment Due notice? Not me, and probably not you either.

This twenties stuff is utter crap.

We are all shooting darts at the bullseye blindfolded.

I can say I've been relatively successful in life.

Successful in the sense that I'm still alive with no preventable ailments and managed to gain a few accolades along the way.

For example, I've moved to New York and did not end up sleeping on a park bench and bumming on the subway. See? Success.

I have a degree and managed to graduate with honors. Success.

I've made it to 26 with no kids. Success. No offense to anyone, but I'm sure at this point in my story you see why me making it this far is a success. If not stop here, do not pass go, do not collect $200. Go back and reread.

Anyway, all of this success is relative. Inconsequential. Sort-of.

On a scale of awful, see *Love and Hip Hop* (pick a city, it really doesn't matter) to queen of the world Beyoncé, I'd say I'm Lauryn Hill after her tax crisis. Not destitute and completely out of the game but shorty has to a lot of work to do to get back to the top.

I mean, I finally moved out of my jail cell of a room in Harlem. No really, it was a cell, I'm not exaggerating. If my brothers, who are all over six feet tall, were to spread their arms their fingers would touch the walls. When I laid on the floor horizontally, I was only a few inches away from touching both walls. It was a box; I know for a fact that prison cells are bigger. Aside from moving, I also started my website and have had a lot of positive responses and support. I've met great people and a few celebrities on the way. According to some, *"New York is treating you right girl!"* The phrase I hear every time I go home. New York treats me a way, I'm just not sure it's the right way. I mean I've had some of my worst experiences here.

One fascinating thing about NYC is the interaction between extreme wealth and extreme poverty. There is constant contact between the two it is unreal to witness. Wealthy women and men on the subway riding to work or an event next to a homeless person with their entire life's worth in a metal shopping cart. I've been in subways with the homeless asking for change, it's a regular occurrence. So much so that there are a few people you begin to recognize. You know their entire speech by heart and sometimes doubt the validity of it. Then there are times when someone comes in and you feel their poverty. It's in their bones that they need help, and I try to give what I can, if I have anything. I've been asked for change and had nothing to give, thinking *I'm really only a nickel and a bad decision away from where they are.* Okay, that's a tad dramatic but I've been asked by homeless for money and literally had $2 in my bank account and was desperately waiting for my next check. I've been eating peanut butter and jelly for the last few weeks, counting change at the bodega to buy a loaf of bread for $2.50. I've been hungry, praying that the office has a meeting with catered lunch so I can eat. From sucking my bank account dry to bed bugs and rats in my home, to being robbed, if some of my best moments have taken place in NYC I can say for a fact that my worst moments of life have too. Ain't no love in the heart of this city.

My biggest fear is that everyone will realize I have no clue what I'm doing. I hope no one finds out. This feeling is apparently universal and has a name: Imposter Syndrome.

Imposter syndrome is very real. Coined by psychologists Dr. Pauline Clance and Suzanne Imes, imposter syndrome refers to high-achieving individuals who are unable to internalize their accomplishments and live with the fear of being exposed as a fraud. Basically, we think what we do don't matter and some kind of way we made it by the hair of our chinny-chin-chin. Even mother Maya was a victim of imposter syndrome. Maya Angelou, a talented poet and all-around artist who lived the epitome of a full life said, *"I have written eleven books, but each time I think, 'uh oh, they're going to find out now. I've run a game on everybody, and they're going to find me out.'"* Knowing one of the greatest of all time too felt like they were clueless helps to salve my scars, alleviate some of the weight pressing down on me. Helps as I write this book, finally finish and publish it- taking a leap I didn't know I would ever make.

I was recently laid off from my job and have been unemployed for nearly seven months. Seven months in NYC and I have no bites, yet. I have applied for jobs in the black hole that is the corporate website, we all know the murky abyss that is online applications. I have added people on LinkedIn, sent cold emails, and asked around my network. Still nada. I swear I've gained a pound for every rejection email I've received. It is times like these where I really feel alone. Where the reality of my life really hits me- that I am in a huge city with no family and few friends. That as much as I have accomplished all of that boils down to who you know that can get you the job you need or want. That it will finally be revealed that I am a fraud. That I've schemed my way to New York and somehow stayed longer than a day. An imposter.

But why do so many of us suffer from imposter syndrome? Part of it is that we constantly compare ourselves to others. We get in the proverbial room and wonder, *"How the heck am I here? What makes me qualified to talk to this person with their fancy title and that person with their talents?"* But you didn't sneak in the room, you didn't bribe a bouncer or slide past security. You were invited for a reason. What's that reason? You have something that someone else saw as important, noticed the value, even if you failed to, or maybe thought no one else would see.

I have to tell myself this daily. That I didn't get here by accident. That it was intentional. Not my being fired, but my intense passion for chasing my dreams and living my life to the best of my ability.

As I continue to figure out this thing called life one thing becomes abundantly clear: no one knows what they are doing. I wish I could give you more than that about navigating your twenties. About the in-between space from college to the rest of your life. Where we wrestle with career, going to school, traveling, balling out, saving money and making all kinds of bad decisions along the way. But I'm still navigating it myself.

26.
Young.
Broke.
Single.

Once this season has ended I might have more concrete answers. But until then, relish in the fact that my life is just as crazy as yours. It can be in shambles one day and full successes the next. Let's just live and enjoy the day. Don't worry about someone else's life, cause worrying about your own is enough, I mean, you just read a snippet of my life and its craziness.

Whether our days be full of lousy bills or amazing opportunities-it will always be glorious because we are here to live it. We've got plenty of time to figure out this thing called life. Promise.

QUARTER CENTURY PART DEUX

Ode to Sallie Mae, and everyone else I owe money to:

Sallie Mae,
I hate you
I wish you'd go away
Trust me
If I had the money
I'd pay

$0.64

(Insert your favorite rap lyrics about getting paid here)

At this point in my life, it seems, I am in a perpetual state of broke. My bank account balance ranging from a small thousandaire to only a couple dollars. On days when my account has four digits I'm on top of the world on days when I have two dollars I'm counting the days to my next paycheck. I've begun to master the art of saving and started investing, looking at ways to build generational wealth- something that's sorely lacking in minority communities. Too often familial deaths only leave debt and those left behind have no idea how to handle it. When I looked at my peers, and as I became one of many young professionals, my mind and vision expanded. I could do much more than live check-to-check, I could amass wealth, enough to take care of my family now and in the future.

Then I started working. No one tells you the fight never ends. Work hard, get a good education and get a job. Those are the three steps many of us were told we needed to follow to be successful in life. That's all you ever heard growing up. Work hard, get a good education and get a job. It was engrained in my mind.

Women on average make 79 cents to every dollar men earn, resulting in a wage gap of 21 percent. Additionally, women of color make even less than 79 cents to every dollar men earn. African-American women make about 64 cents, American Indian and Alaskan Native women make 59 cents while Hispanic and Latin women take home about 54 cents to every dollar. Asian-American women have the smallest pay gap at about 90 percent of men's earnings. For young women, the gap is even higher compared to the earnings of male counterparts of the same age. The statistics are sad and I can say from personal experience they are true.

How would it be if I only showed up to work 64% of the time? I would gladly work less for the pay, but that is not how things works. It's not equal work, equal pay.

My first foray into corporate America I had no real knowledge or understanding of negotiating salary and the inherent biases I would face. I had been in New York for two months and things were finally falling into place for me. I landed a paid internship with an accessory manufacturing company and was proving to the team I was qualified and deserving of a full-time position within the company. By a stroke of grace, the young woman holding the sales assistant position on the team I was interning for resigned to return to school leaving an immediate opening. My direct supervisor was impressed with my work and the vice president of the division liked what he saw. They both considered me for the position. I eagerly accepted and awaited my official offer. This is what I had been waiting for. What I flew halfway across the country for. What I left my family and took a risk for. It was finally happening for me. I could stay in New York and start my career.

When I got my offer letter I saw a proposed wage of $30,000. I called my direct supervisor since she and I had a good rapport. In fact, we still keep in contact today. She has been instrumental in my life for the short time I have known her. She could relate to me, she was a Latina woman who had also taken a risk to make what she wanted in life happen. She was feisty, no really she was, not because she is Latina, but because she did not tolerate foolishness. She would say, *"If I had a dick and balls people would respect what I said, I don't care about my delivery."* I asked her, in confidence, what she thought about my wage and she shared the vice president actually wanted to give me less but she fought for the $30,000. I appreciated her honesty and accepted my offer letter. I mean, what choice did I have? My money I saved to move was drying up, and I had to pay rent to stay in New York. Once I began working and got deep into the company, I learned another sad fact about wage inequalities. The young lady in the role before me was white and Jewish, my company was Jewish owned, and she made $38,000 in the same position. I was shocked and infuriated and I felt cheated, ashamed, and much more. All these emotions tore through me when I found out her wage.

I sucked it up and chopped it up as a loss. But I was sure that when it came time for a promotion I negotiated my butt off to make up for some of the loss. I still wasn't where I was supposed to be but I was glad I made more. Thirty thousand a year could be okay as a single woman in Missouri. Thirty thousand a year in New York City you had to stretch it and really work with I, rent alone could gobble up half of your paycheck.

I was still at the accessory company heading into year three and was ready to leave but finding no success in applications and interviews. Also at this time a new intern had arrived, the first since my internship. He was a recent college graduate, like I had been, looking to start his career. That is where our similarities ended. His uncle was president at another major company and friends with the chief financial officer of mine. *See where this headed?* Despite not being the best intern he was offered a job and became a full-time employee. I didn't even want to know his salary as I'm sure it would add insult to injury. This information is not to assassinate him. He was nice, privileged and white. We got along well and joked about the craziness that was work and other coworkers, but I knew if we did not work together we would have likely never held a conversation. We were from different worlds. His life had a trajectory for company presidential status, without him even having to purposely set out for that type of success. His presence was fuel to my fire reminding me that so often it's not ability, skill, or astuteness that will get you the job but simply who you know.

After praying and fasting I had decided to quit. Then I got laid off, a blessing in disguise. I'd tell you where I ended up next but as I write this the job hunt continues...

In the words of the famous songstress Robyn "Rihanna" Fenty, *Bitch Better Have My Money*. If you learn nothing else from my situation, and the stories of others, know you may need to fight for every dollar you earn.

Equip yourself with the necessary tools to negotiate your salary. Here are my salary negotiating tips from my first foray into earning my worth:

1. **Know your worth.** Research median salaries for exact and similar positions in your area. The median wage for a store manager in Los Angeles is not the same as in Little Rock, Arkansas. Know what others are making and determine what you want your desired salary to be. Remember, you have to live off of this money.

2. **Aim high.** Employers usually will lowball you, so start your negotiation higher than what you actually want. This way you can work to settle somewhere in the middle, which will likely get the salary you want or close to it.

3. **Speak up and be open to negotiation**. You were chosen for a reason. When negotiating salary be able to articulate why you should be given this wage. If it helps have your research regarding median salaries for positions with the same responsibilities and tasks you will be doing. Don't fear the negotiation, embrace it. Think strategically and don't take it

personally, it's business and *YOU CAN DO THIS!*

4. **Its not just your salary.** When determining your wages, depending on your industry, your offer letter may also state terms regarding bonuses and any additional income. Look into how your bonus is structured. Is your bonus guaranteed or based on performance? What determines the amount? You can also negotiate your bonus terms, and even your vacation days before you accept an offer letter. You only get one opportunity to secure everything before you sign on so be confident in everything you are agreeing to.

5. **Pick your battles.** Decide what you want to haggle over and what you can live with. If you are just starting and experience is more important, go with the initial offer, it is your decision. If you are a seasoned expert, and have the resume to prove it, demand what you're worth, and if the company wants you, they will pay. You must know your strengths and be able to determine what you are willing to accept or sacrifice.

Remember, you are worth it. Don't fear demanding what you are worth. I know it is an uphill battle, but it is yet another one I believe we cannot afford to fight- literally and figuratively.

WHEN MOURNING COMES

I am here today because somebody prayed for me —
My grandmother
Sacrificed and prayed for me
Unselfishly, unceasingly

Three suitcases.
Empty pockets.
And a broken heart.

That's what I arrived in New York City with on the cold snowy March night. I was sad, hopeful, fearful, anxious, nervous and more. There are millions of words to describe the bevy of emotions that went through me at that moment. I had never been to New York before. I was here, officially, without a clue what I would do. I was going to attempt to work in fashion. My life would finally start. Maybe? I had my laptop and my childhood stuffed animal tucked safely on my body; I refused to trust the airline with something so precious. As I collected my three suitcases from the carousel and navigated my way to the taxi line, my mind and body were exhausted while simultaneously humming with anxiousness. The east coast was experiencing a late winter storm and snow dropped on me as I waited in line. There were about six people ahead of me. I slowly crept to the front of the line and met the attendant directing travelers to which car to go to.

"Where ya headed?" he asked looking down at his pad.

I really wasn't sure where I was headed, in life, or the location of the temporary housing I secured. I think I mumbled Manhattan, I'm pretty sure I knew I was living in Manhattan, whatever that meant. I pulled out my phone for the address.

The attendant pointed me to a taxi, and I loaded my luggage into the trunk. The driver asked the same thing, "Where ya headed?" I read him the address. He entered the address into his GPS and proceeded to chauffeur me off into the darkness, carrying me to the unknown ahead.

The day before I took off into the unknown my grandmother died.

My grandmother died and I am in New York City.

***

The previous day I woke up to the hospital calling. The caller on the phone said, "Your grandmother is not doing well and we need someone from the family to come to the hospital." My heart dropped, I knew, but I refused to believe it. Why else would they speak so cryptically? Bobby sat in his corner chair and looked at me as I stood in the living room on the house phone. I told him what the caller said. I rushed back to the room I shared with my cousin Julia and threw on some clothes and shoes.

"Slow down Relly, take your time," he said.

I was nervous and anxious. "I'll call you when I get there," I quickly rambled and left.

It was raining.

I remember looking through the splattered windshield thinking: she's dead. An entire inner dialogue on endless loop during my drive. *No, she can't be dead. It's not real. But she must be. Something's wrong. Hospitals only give cryptic calls like that when something is wrong. I've watched enough movies and read enough books to know that. Right?*

Memories of her assault me left and right as I make my way to the hospital.

***

I'm a kid again. Somewhere between girl and woman. Body becoming woman while mind is still blissfully full of unvanquished fantasies.

Grandma and I are in the kitchen making breakfast. Nothing fancy just scrambled eggs, bacon, and biscuits. The kitchen smells good, as usual, and the house is buzzing with Saturday morning activity.

The cast iron skillet, that is older than everyone in the house, sits on the stove with bacon sizzling and crackling to crispy brown perfection. My great-great grandmother cooked on that skillet. Grandma says it's well-seasoned, whatever that means. I know it's big and black and we use it for just about everything.

I try to open the biscuit can without flinching, but that expected pop gets me every time. I place the soft sticky white dough on the baking sheet and under grandma's watchful eye I put them in the oven.

She cracks the eggs and lets me season them with pepper and whisk with a fork.

After placing the crunchy bacon on a plate covered with paper towels, to soak up the grease, we pour the eggs in the skillet next. I try to steal a piece of bacon when grandma's back is turned. It's so good and it leaves my fingertips shiny with grease.

The eggs are done, and it's time for everybody to eat. We always make grandpa's plate first then it's time for everyone else to come in and make their food.

I pull out a paper plate and a plastic holder for my grandma to fix my grandpa's plate so I can take it up to him. While she makes his plate, I reach in the cabinet for his hot sauce, his requisite for every meal. I turn and accept the now filled plate.

"Grandma there's no eggs on here," I say.

"Yo grandpa said he don't like my eggs," she says haughtily, a matter of fact claim not to be disputed. At this point in my life, my grandparents have been together for over twenty years.

"I made him a plate one day, and he looked at me and said 'wife, you know, I never really liked your eggs,' I been cooking for him for years, so fuck him. I ain't cooking no more eggs for him again. He can starve for all I care."

I can't help but laugh out loud. My grandpa is crazy and so is my grandma. *How has he been eating scrambled eggs he don't like for so long?* And I know grandma is serious, she'll never scramble him another egg.

I say nothing else, but grandpa likes my eggs.

***

When I arrived at the hospital, the first person I saw was my aunt Irene in her wheelchair. My cousin, Justin, was there too, they went to church together that morning. I missed my last service at my childhood church before I moved to NYC. Did I miss it or did the call stop me from going? I don't remember, and now it doesn't matter. I asked my aunt what happened, and she said my grandma's heart gave out and the staff had been trying to resuscitate her. I cried. I don't even think my mind had caught up to what my body instinctively knew to do, which was mourn. I cried and cried. And as more family arrived, the news shared one by one, it was painful.

My cousin was at work.

"Julia, do I call her and tell her?"

"She can't do anything from work, don't call her," my aunt answers as we sit in the lobby. A dejected group not sure what to do or how to do it, the death real and unreal at the same time. God bless my mother. She handles crises like no other. It must be from her being a mother. All of my type-A personality that knows to focus on prioritizing tasks seemed to have left out the window with my grandmother's soul.

My brothers.

None of them were there. Anytime something happens they are the first ones I think about. I worry how they will take it. I want to be with them when they get the news. I love them, sometimes too much.

I hate hospitals. Pretty much always have. I've spent a decent amount of time in them, though I've only been a patient once. Due to asthma complications, I spent a few days at the children's hospital to be monitored. I was about 6 or 7 and it was a kiddie vacation. I was waited on and got to eat whatever I wanted. I had my own room and television to watch cartoons. I didn't have my brothers driving me crazy, and I didn't have to share. Everything in my hospital room was mine. It was paradise. The only time I could ever call a hospital paradise. It wasn't paradise when my grandmother was sick the entire summer my junior year of college. It wasn't paradise when they carried pieces of my grandmother away one by one. First a toe. Then another toe. Then the next toe. Then the entire bottom leg. It wasn't paradise when my grandfather had a stroke. Followed by a heart attack. It wasn't paradise when my aunt's kidneys failed. It wasn't paradise when she was put on dialysis in her mid-thirties. I hate hospitals. I hate the smells. I hate the sounds. I hate how sterile they are, cold and hard with no softness in sight. I hate them because they signify bad news. They signify death. They remind me of my mortality.

Death scares me. My grandmother was never scared of dying. She welcomed it like she embraced tomorrow or a good meal. It was part of her life. She even had shoes purchased, never worn, that she planned to be buried in. A pair of gaudy clear heels with a gold lion on the side and a mesh-covered front. As a kid, I tried them on and broke one strap, and never told her, cause I knew they were her funeral shoes. *Her funeral shoes.* Sounds crazy right? But that was my grandma, a true OG in life and death. Me, on the other hand, my mortality frightens me. Heaven is great, exciting even, but the way I may end up there is not comforting. How will you die? In your sleep, an accident, a killing, the possibilities are endless.

That day at the hospital was everything I hated wrapped in one. Smells, overwhelming sterilization, unpleasing sounds and death. *"Do you want to see the body before they move it?"* we were asked by the chaplain or a doctor. I'm not sure. It doesn't matter. We all say yes. I get up and go to the room around the corner and see my grandmother. She looks sleep. Her body still adjusting to death, it hasn't taken hold yet. Her skin still brown. I awkwardly lean over and hug the body and it makes a sound. I thought she would wake up but I know it's part of the death process. Bodies still do things once the soul has left. I'm awkwardly affectionate so my hug to her dead body was just that, awkward.

My Aunt Kate and Uncle Rainbow, that's his nickname, everyone on my grandpa's side has a nickname, went to pick up my grandpa before they came to the hospital. I don't even know my uncle Rainbow's real name, as a matter of fact, I don't know many of my uncles or aunts' government names on my grandpa's side of the family. Some nicknames include Bud, Frog, Moose and Honeycomb. Don't ask where the names come from. They're black, country folks and I love them. My grandpa didn't want to get up and get dressed. He was always cantankerous, but the stroke made it worst. My grandfather is a television character. I would have made millions putting him on screen, of this, I have no doubt. He is obnoxiously rude, honest, sarcastic and a drunk. He has no filter and his commentary is legendary. He suffered brain damage and did not commit to rehabilitation. I don't need a doctor to tell me what I know. He's not the same.

They didn't want to tell him why he had to get up, but they had to in order to get him to the hospital. I am out of her room in the hall and my grandpa limps to her room on a cane. He is so small. After his stroke, he lost so much weight. He suffers so much now. He was the only "healthy" one in the family and his decay has been quick and severe. He goes in the room and they sit him in the chair next to my grandmother. He is slightly hunched over and he is crying. No, he is sobbing. Deep gut wrenching sobs I've never seen before. He grabs her lifeless hand on the bed and with his other hand removes his glasses. He has snot running down his nose. If I ever doubted their love before I won't ever again. *"That is love,"* I think to myself. *"He loved her so much. They were in love. What do you do?"* I see his sobbing silhouette from my position in the hall and it all becomes even more real for me.

My grandmother is dead. She is gone.

I'm supposed to fly to New York tomorrow morning. I don't know what to do.

I volunteer to pick up my cousin to tell her the news.

Memories assault my conscience again.

***

A few weeks ago, Julia and I went to church with my grandmother. We sat in the pew while she sat next to us in her wheelchair. The sermon was great and much needed. I looked over and grandma was crying. The sermon was good, but I didn't think it warranted tears.

After church ended she introduced us to some of the members she formed relationships with. This was a new church home for her so she only knew a few people. My childhood church down the street yet worlds away. She was making her new spiritual home here. We all had moved on. We were introduced to a woman with a daughter named Julia, an older woman with her energetic grandson and a few other members.

When we got home, I talked to grandma about why she was crying. We had gotten into an argument earlier over something silly. Prompting more waterworks as I feigned an apology. I've never like crying, from myself or others. She cried, "I'm going to miss you when you leave for NYC."

Sunday worship and tears. I hugged her, salty wetness clinging to my neck and chin, unsure of any other way to provide comfort.

"I just thought how blessed I was. To be sitting at church with my two beautiful granddaughters right next to me. It made me happy. I'm proud of you two young women."

***

I pick my cousin up. Tell her with an awkward face that tries to smile to soften the blow. She doesn't believe it for a second, then she does. She cries and I cry trying to comfort her. We ride home in silence, it's all we know right now.

That evening the house is full of people. That's what happens when someone dies. People come around. To feed you. Console you. Check on the family. People. People. People. Everywhere. I go to my shared room and call my dad. I'm sobbing the entire time, "She's gone. And now I'm worried about Bobby. People usually die within a year of their spouse's death. Great Grandpa died a year after Great Grandma. And I'm supposed to fly to New York tomorrow. I don't know what to do." That's me, always worried about something. Thinking ahead. Too logical for my own good sometimes.

My dad tries to calm me down. "You know what you need to do. New York will always be there. You need to be with your family now. They need you. Your brothers need you."

My mom says something similar in the kitchen surrounded by women. Women from church, her job, her scrapbook group. I need to be here she tells me. You know what you need to do she says. She drapes it with love just like my dad. A parent's love can be so strong its tangible, maybe even suffocating with its vice-like grip.

They're right though, I need to be here.

My aunt calls me into her room. She's been in and out of her room. In and out of mourning. It's an out-of-body experience, hovering between what was and what is, not yet settled in this new reality. She's been in between crying fits and normalcy like the rest of us. It's still surreal. She's not crying at the moment but the room is dark, she's sitting in her chair with the lights off.

"You need to go to New York," she says this firmly. "I hear my mother clear as day telling me to tell you to go. You had a good relationship with her. Y'all were close. There is no unfinished business or loose strings."

She says I should go and I listen. She has been with me these past six months while I saved and worked out housing arrangements. Figuring out where to stay and the cost of living. While the people and family in the house question the decision, and me, she says what she told me and adds, which is true, my living situation is too precarious so I need to go now while it's secured. My aunt adds, "If she doesn't go now she may never go."

If I don't go now I may never go.

I call my friend Symone and ask her to take me to the airport. In all the chaos I have no ride there, she says of course. She meets me the next morning at my house. I have my three suitcases packed. More people are at the house. I see family I haven't seen in a while, some in years. I hug them and tell them I am leaving for New York. People already think I'm crazy leaving for New York with no job, they have to think I'm certified psychotic for leaving now when my grandmother just died.

I walk through the house and head to my grandpa, sitting in his living room chair. I hug him and he begins to cry. I cry too. "Be safe. Know you can always come home," he says through tears. "You can always come home."

I cry and tell him bye and his words have always stayed in my head and heart to this day. No matter what happens to me in New York City, or anywhere, *I can always go home. I can always go home.*

I cry to the airport taking final looks at the only city I have called home for the past 22 years. We arrive, park and lug my bags to the terminal. I hug Symone goodbye and get in line to check-in and take off into the unknown.

Three suitcases.
Empty pockets.
And a broken heart.
I'm headed to New York City. What will happen to me?

FIN

Funny that this last passage you read was the first one I wrote. I've always had a thing about endings. I notoriously read the last sentence, if not page, of every book I read before even beginning the story. I don't mind movie spoilers as long as they don't ruin the entire plot. I like to know how things end. It determines if it's worth my time. Worth my investment. Worth my energy. Boy, does God have different plans. In this life I can never know the end, this is a challenge for me. I told you; I like to know how it ends before I decide to start. In every aspect of my life I've had to move without seeing the final destination, going to my chosen college, moving to New York, writing this book. I have no idea if I will be successful or fail, but I do know that I must move in order to find out. I have learned that I am much more afraid of staying in the same place than I am of the unknown. Stagnation breeds the same outcome each time, once you learn to accept this fact you can move.

Move to learn.
Move to grow.
Move to love yourself- fat, black, nappy and all of that other -ish. I can't promise a happy ending but I can promise it'll be one heck of a ride.
You ready?

Buckle up.

AFTERWORD

As I've grown so has the world and the black renaissance happening now is beautiful and wonderful and spectacular to watch. I love seeing how many women are claiming ownership of themselves- mind, body, and soul. It is great to witness, and know, that we will raise our daughters and sons with the mentality that black is beautiful, smart, bold, powerful, soft, sweet, and everything else, it's glorious.

To know my niece is growing up being taught to embrace herself brings me joy. I love that she is growing learning her hair is beautiful and that she's enough as she is. I envy that, but more than envy I am filled with warmth and happiness that the future generation of my family will hopefully love themselves wholly, that maybe the path to self-discovery won't have as many potholes, bumps, and wrong turns to get there.

Me, I'm still trying to live and blend two worlds- the woman who knows her worth and value and the girl who never loved herself. I look back at old pictures and I don't recognize myself. My posture conveyed the fears I felt inside, deeply slouching trying to make myself smaller. Photos now show a woman growing into herself, claiming her space in the world. She's no longer shrinking.

***

I still struggle.
I struggle daily.
With my insecurities.
With being vulnerable enough to be open, but wise enough to avoid foolish decisions.
I still grow.
I grow daily.
Each day I get a little stronger.
Better equipped at tackling life.
Learn something new.
Change my mind.
Take a chance.
We are ever evolving.
Changing.
Resurrecting from our former selves.
The way nature intended it.

ACKNOWLEDGEMENTS

Thank you God for always reminding me whose path I'm on and to trust in Your timing- what's meant for me will be. I am learning that I am worthy of Your grace and working to accept it daily.

To my parents, I love you. Thank you for your unconditional love. Thank you for raising me and giving me independence. Thank you for my crazy siblings. Without you there is no me and I hope I make you proud every day.

Aunt Irene, thank you for being the one to push me from the nest, without which I would have never discovered I can fly.

My brothers, Darrell, E'saias, Preston, Christian, and Christopher, I do it all for you. You all are the reason I strive, the reason I try. I refuse to let you down and hope I can make your lives easier one day.

Jamison, my sister, I love you.

To my family, and friends I consider family, I love you all. You are with me every day. You'll never know the lessons each of you have left me and the memories I hold dear. Family, I never take our legacy for granted.

Thank you to my friends. I'm a hard one to love yet you all do.

Thanks to my friend Cassondra Lenoir for sharing your self-publishing experience with me and knowing there is no such thing as competition.

Special thank you to my friend Britney Thompson, a talented all-around artist, who willingly shared her gift to create the cover art and bring my vision to life.

Thank you to Cyril Trinidad, my cover designer, who always comes through in the clutch. You know I appreciate you.

My early readers, Chasity Cooper and Shawnette "ShawnG" George, thank you for taking a chance on me. I appreciate your feedback, edits and most importantly your time. For time is a gift and I am glad you shared it with me and *Nappy by Nature*.

Proverbs 11: 24-25 (MSG) *The world of the generous gets larger and larger; the world of the stingy gets smaller and smaller. The one who blesses others is abundantly blessed; those who help others are helped.* The Nappy by Nature financial contributors, that helped make this a reality, I wish you blessings as you have sowed into my life: Angela Gilmore-Taylor, Yvonne Chamberlain, Dayanne Danier, and Jasmine Barbour.

Grandma Melanie, I know you always wanted to write a book and though my stories aren't nearly as exciting as yours, I hope you look down at me and find joy in the stories and lessons from you I've shared. Through me–and the family–you live, with these pages you live eternally. I love you.

Last, but definitely not least, to the readers of this book thank you for allowing me to be vulnerable. Find your strength, find your voice and when you do don't shut up for anyone. It is my hope for you, as for me, "*to be the person who you needed when you were younger.*" I am wishing you endless miracles and blessings.

ABOUT THE AUTHOR

Like many millennials, Charell Strong currently works in corporate America while actively pursuing and discovering her entrepreneurial dreams and passions. She has worked with several high profile brands and has written for CRWN Magazine. She is founder of the minority women empowerment and lifestyle website Strong and Elite with the motto "She Dares to Exist." Nappy by Nature is her first published work, and she is now officially claiming the title writer.

Charell is from Kansas City, Missouri, not Kansas, and currently lives in New York City. Charell moved to New York City with no job lined up or previous visits to the big city. She is no stranger to fear and taking the proverbial jump into the unknown. It's her constant embracing of fear, instead of letting it deter her, that helps her success. Charell is still out learning and navigating this thing called life and embracing every moment of it.

Connect with her on the internet @charelliam everywhere or visit her website charellstrong.com.

Made in the USA
Middletown, DE
20 February 2017